# Circle of Song

## Songs, Chants, and Dances for Ritual and Celebration

by
**Kate Marks**

# Circle of Song

## Songs, Chants, and Dances for Ritual and Celebration

First Edition, Full Circle Press  P.O. Box 428, Amherst, M.A.  01004

© 1993 All Rights Reserved. Second Printing, 1995 Revised

Book Design–Barkat Curtin, Spring Hill Graphics
Illustrations–Jan Billings and Jeanette Gawry Perman
Cover Concept–Kate Marks, based on a photograph by Mary Durland
Cover Art–SH Graphics
Cover Design–Barkat Curtin, Terence Fehr
Printed and bound by Malloy Lithographing, Inc, Ann Arbor, MI

Library of Congress Catalog Number  93-73300
ISBN  0-9637489-O-41

**FULL CIRCLE PRESS**

# Dedication

To the singer, dancer and ceremonialist in us all.

This book is dedicated to my family and especially to the memory of my grandfather,
E. B. Marks, well known songwriter of his day, who exactly 100 years ago
started his own successful music publishing company.

# Acknowledgements

This book has been a work of dedication and love over many years. I want to thank the many many people who have helped me along the way:

The staff at Findhorn Press (especially Sandra Kramer) who were originally going to publish the book and provided the initial inspiration, funding and creative work on the project.
Bill Whiteaker, Mark Rose, Katherine Klein, Marilyn Penn, Barbara Swetina and most particularly Bill St.Clair for their many hours of music transcribing.
Gina Gold and Majida Gibson for their sharp editing skills.
Jan Billings and Gawry Perman for the beautiful illustrations.
Alan Hayes for the index and appendices.
Becky Drees for paste up
Terence Fehr and Alan Hayes for the cover
Especially to Barkat Curtin (Springhill Graphics)
and
Alan Hayes (S–H Graphics)
for their countless hours of invaluable help and support with typesetting, layout, design, computer consultation, general feedback and morale boosting.

Finally, to the many people who have shared their songs and chants over the years .

**Thank you all, I am deeply grateful.**

# Table of Contents

# Introduction

*If you can walk*
*You can dance*
*If you can talk*
*You can sing*

—Saying from Zimbabwe

Sacred music and dance are powerful tools that have been used by cultures throughout the ages to awaken consciousness, call in power, heal the body and spirit and enhance the celebration of important occasions. For the ancients, dance and music were considered not just for entertainment but as forms of active prayer and worship, a way of communing with the gods and goddesses, of re-connecting with the cycles of nature and with all life.

Today in the West, many people have forgotten the true purpose of these arts. We need to reclaim our ancient dance/music heritage, to revive and create sacred music and dance forms that are appropriate for our lives today.

This ceremonial sourcebook offers chants, songs, dances, simple rituals and meditations to enhance our communion with the sacred and help us celebrate with others. The material is presented by themes along with other text and guidelines to inspire individual and group creativity.

## The Power of Chanting

Sound, especially the human voice is a powerful catalyst for healing and transformation. As we sound and sing, we harmonize our being, lift our spirits and dissolve our pain.

Unlike a song, a chant usually consists of only a few words and a simple melody that can be readily learned and easily repeated. Because of this repetitive quality, chants put us quickly into a meditative state and help us to easily clear and center our minds. A chant is designed to activate and balance the inner self, to amplify and raise energy and focus spiritual power. As we chant the words and melody repetitively, we give voice to our feelings, deepen our devotion, and call forth what we want into our lives. Every chant has a specific purpose and meaning associated with it that can be invoked each time it is sung. A chant accumulates power with each repetition. It helps us to become one-pointed in our concentration; to quiet and empty our active thinking minds and connect deeply with the core of our being. The simpler and more repetitive the chant, the more effective it is. Repetition puts us easily in a hypnotic state where we no longer have to think about what we are singing; the chant begins to work through us. We are no longer doing the singing, the singing is doing us.

Often a chant incorporates a key inspirational, sacred phrase called a mantra in Sanskrit. The word 'man', means to meditate or contemplate, and 'tra' means to protect and free from bondage. These sacred phrases include the names of God/Goddess, prayers, poems and other inspirational thoughts upon which we can meditate, bringing us closer to spirit, to ourselves and all life. Mantras are chanted over and over, either aloud or silently, helping us to attune to a particular vibration, deity or energy we want to bring into our lives. An effective mantra or chant stays with us and reverberates in our mind throughout the day. It brings us increasing balance and harmony and creates a deep trance state which can last for hours.

Many sacred phrases in chants are affirmations. They invoke a particular quality we want to affirm or call into our lives, such as 'Air I am, Fire I am'. Some of the choruses of our popular songs have become mantras. For example, the well-known 'We Shall Overcome' or the familiar Beatles 'Let it be' repeated over and over are forms of mantra. Saying and singing them out loud gives them more power—especially when we repeat them over and over. Through chants and songs we plant positive thoughts and ideas which are then quickly made emotional through music. The feeling evoked by music magnifies words. Psychologists have found that music works much faster than affirmations or the spoken word alone for programming our subconscious.

The most powerful mantras and sacred phrases are in ancient languages such as Hebrew and Sanskrit. We feel the vibration of the sounds reverberating within us, even if we do not know their meanings. But it is also important for us today to use and empower our own modern languages, to bring sacredness to our everyday words.

Chanting is active vocal prayer. As we chant, we sharpen our focus and intention and deepen our devotion. For example, many Native American chants begin with 'Hey'. As we say 'Hey' we call the divine forces and say 'I want your attention.' Calling also gives us a way to work with affirmations—naming and claiming what we want. Not only are we affirming that 'I am—', we actively invoke and call that quality or thing.

## Working with Chants

Chants, simple songs and dances, such as the ones in this book, are wonderful to use as part of personal and group rituals and ceremonies. They help us to focus intention, build community and bond quickly with others. When a group makes sounds or music together, a vibrational force field is created which accelerates and intensifies the healing process.

As you sing, it is good to attune to the essential quality and power of the chant, to feel its unique spirit and vibration. Some chants work best if sung in a strong, steady, sustained voice all the way through. Others need to be sung slowly, still others more quickly. Stay with the feeling evoked by the words and music. Whenever your mind wanders, especially when doing a repetitive mantra, come back to the feeling. Let the feeling deepen.

Before chanting, try a preparatory meditation. (See examples of meditations throughout the text.) Or experiment with the following wordless free form vocal toning exercises, to help open up your voice, and release sounds spontaneously.

## Vocal Exercises:

### Humming

- Become aware of your breathing. As you exhale, allow a soft sustained hum to emerge, centered in your heart.

- As you hum, envision yourself as a happy cat purring. Release a hum of deep joy, and satisfaction, as in 'Mmmmmmmm, good!'

- Let the hum expand and move through you, waking up any parts of your body that are asleep or resistant. Feel as if you are giving yourself an internal sound massage.

- Gradually become aware of others around you and blend your humming with theirs. Continue until you feel calm and centered. When you are ready, open your eyes.

### Toning — Opening Your Voice·

- Focus on your breath. Breathe in through the nose and out through the mouth. Then, as you exhale, begin to make a sighing sound, releasing any tension. Gradually let the sigh develop into long, open vowel sounds such as the sound AH or OH. Continue to sigh and then open your voice expressing freely. Direct your tones into different parts of your body.

- Continue to watch your breath and bring your awareness and sound into your heart. Let your unique heartsong emerge and grow.

- If you are in a group, listening to others is key. Notice how your voice blends with the others. Express your unique sounds, but stay in harmony with the group sounds.

- Experiment with feeling as if you are a lead instrument in a great improvisational symphony. Alternate between being fully aware of your own body and voice and then of the blending of your sound with the group. As you sing, really listen to the others. Unite your collective hearts and souls. Chanting and dancing can lead to states of ecstasy, but it is important to stay conscious of the earth and your body while letting yourself experience higher states.

One of the most powerful chants to work with, especially for beginnings and endings, is the ancient universal sound of OM. (A U M). As you chant it at least three times, you will experience it vibrating your whole body/being. Focus initially on your lower body with the O and then be aware of the sound rising up until you experience the M resonating at the top of your head. Some women's groups prefer to chant MA instead of OM. This is the universal call of the mother. As you chant MA, experience the energy descending from the top of your head on the M and into the heart center on the AH.

## Building and Sustaining Power Through Chanting

The following chanting techniques will help you build up energy, call in spiritual power and sharpen your focus and intention:

- Start the chant slowly, gradually building up its power and intensity, so it is sung louder, faster, or in a strong, sustained voice.

- As you repeat the chant, pour your feelings, and intentions into each word.

- Allow the chant to reach a peak, feeling its energy rise higher and higher; your focus growing stronger. Add body movement, ecstatic dancing.

- Finally, slow the chant down. Let it get softer, and stop gradually.

- To end, ground yourself well. For example, imagine roots extending deep into the earth from the bottoms of your feet. Or bend over and connect with the earth, bringing your hands and/or head to the ground. You can also make sure you are back in your body by patting yourself in a few places or clapping your hands.

## Musical Accompaniment

Keep the accompaniment simple; the simpler the better. A strong drumbeat or rattle shake that accentuates the natural rhythm of the chant or mantra works best; or play simple guitar or piano chords. Add other simple, easy to use instruments such as percussion and bells. Let the power of the chant or song be foremost. Chants are often more powerful when they are sung unaccompanied.

## The Drone

Another suggestion is to accompany the chant with a simple drone sound. The drone is done by repetitively playing or singing one long sustained note, a series of sustained notes or an open chord. This helps us to calm and center our minds, to become one–pointed as we explore one note in depth. Drone music is found in cultures the world over. In

India there is the tamboura, and harmonium; in Spain there is flamenco. Irish and Scottish music is often built on simple modes and uses the droning bagpipes. Our own Appalachian folk music, played on the banjo and dulcimer, is also full of drone sounds. We can make drone sounds with our voices through humming, toning and chanting.

**Drumming**

Drumming is one of the most ancient, powerful ways to accompany chants, dances and ritual. The drum is round; it is a feminine form which awakens our instinctual earthy nature as well as ancient images and symbols. The drum is used to carry and sustain the energy, to keep the inner pulse; it echoes the heartbeat of Mother Earth and of all life.

In shamanism, the hypnotic rhythmic beat of the drum is most commonly used to provide movement, momentum and a point of focus for inner journeys. Shamans refer to the drum as the horse or the canoe, because it is used as a vehicle to travel to the spirit world. Drumming is said to be most effective for inducing trance states when the beat is synchronized at a frequency of between four and seven impulses per second. This is the same frequency as theta waves in the brain, the wavelength associated with dreams and visionary states.

Many of the meditations and inner journeys in this book lend themselves to drum accompaniment. Ideally, have one person drum for you or use a taped version of the drumming. (See appendix for more information on drumming tapes, where to get drums and how to make your own drum.) You can also read any instructions before beginning an inner journey so that you absorb most of what you need to know. This will allow the drumbeat to continue without words. Most important is that you feel safe, supported and deepened as you journey into an altered state.

The simplest drum to use is a round frame drum with a beater. If you are more experienced, experiment with other drums such as the Middle Eastern dumbek, or African congas, djembe, etc. Rattles, sticks, and bells are also good.

The drummer needs to be able to keep a steady even beat and be sensitive to the energy of the group process. She/he needs to know how to listen and follow the group pulse, in order to support what is happening, rather than becoming a distraction. This is not the place for fancy drum rhythms, improvisation, and solo acts. If the basic heartbeat stops, the energy will drop immediately. This may be what is called for at certain times. At other times it may be appropriate to gradually speed up the tempo to raise the energy, or to slow it down to ground the energy.

Larger group drums, known as Mother drums, are often used by communities and dance circles. These drums usually sit on a stand and are played by up to eight persons. The following is an example of a simple drum ceremony using a Mother Drum:

### Drumming Ceremony

- Gather around a group drum and/or sit in a circle with your individual drums and other percussion instruments.

- Select a drum leader; someone who can hold a steady beat which will remain constant throughout. (If there is a group drum, the leader should use this.)

- Decide how long you want to drum. Your ceremony can last a short time or go on for hours, even days. Always have at least two people holding the beat at all times, so that others can rest at intervals.

- Before beginning, the leader says a prayer of dedication for the drumming ceremony—to Mother Earth, World Peace, or for the healing of a person, the group, or a particular issue. An offering of tobacco or cornmeal is made to the drum. Then the leader begins the heartbeat.

- After the heartbeat is strong and even, others can join in with their individual drums and percussion instruments as they feel the rhythm. Counter rhythms can be played as long as the heartbeat is kept central. Generally, the mother drum keeps a steady beat with each beat being of equal length. The drummer(s) can also imitate the actual heart beat using a short and long pattern: short—long—pause, short—long—pause.

- It is important for everybody to keep their focus and intention clear, to listen deeply, staying sensitive and attuned to each other. Imagine the heartbeat coming from deep in the earth, vibrating with the universal rhythm of life, as well as your own heartbeat.

- Add voices, chants, dances, and other instruments in an organic flowing process.

- If the rhythm changes, let everyone listen and return to the single beat of the Heart drum until the energies/sounds harmonize.

- To end the ceremony, the leader comes into the center of the circle and signals to the group. This can be arranged at the beginning, perhaps counting the last four beats out loud. The final beat is struck strongly, with everyone together.

- End in silence, absorbing the vibrations and integrating your experience. Share verbally around the circle if you wish. Hold hands, and say appropriate closing prayers.

### Rattles

Rattles, like the drum, are powerful ritual tools. They are usually made of dried gourds with seeds (pebbles, beans or small crystals) placed inside for the sound. When the rattle is shaken, the seeds are brought to life. The gourds are attached to a stick and decorated with one's personal symbols of power. The rattling sound is thought to open up the doorway into the spirit world, to call our spirit guides, allies and guardians to us.

Rattles are also used to heighten our intention, to focus and direct energy. You can rattle to create sacred space or to send healing energy into a sick person's body. When you shake the rattle up and down, you call in active, masculine energy; when you shake it side to side you invoke receptive, more feminine energy.

## Guidelines For Sharing Chants with Others

- Try to get everyone to participate, especially those who are inhibited and feel that they cannot sing or dance. This will help unify and attune the group.

- Know the song well enough yourself so you are comfortable teaching it. As you show confidence in your voice, you will draw in others and build enthusiasm.

- Sing the melody several times with the group until it becomes familiar. Then add the words, extra verses and harmony.

- Make sure the group understands the meaning of the words. Repeat the words several times, especially if there are more than four lines. Print them out if possible.

- Encourage everyone to sing from their hearts and feel the essence of what they are singing. Experiment with evoking different moods— slow, sad, fast, happy or melancholy. Try changing the beat, the pitch and the dynamics; repeat the chant for a while in a whisper, or silently (on the breath). This deepens your experience. Be aware of the quality of the chant — is it sharp, gentle, calming, stimulating? Notice how the higher notes connect you more to your upper body and spirit, while the lower notes go deep into your body, helping you connect with the earth.

- At times, you may want just the women to sing, or just the men.

- Repeat familiar chants and gradually add new ones.

- Don't be afraid to stop a chant or dance if it just isn't making it. It is more important to bring the group into harmony than to do the chant/dance all the way through without group focus and cohesion.

- Many of the chants can be sung as rounds. Rounds are a good way to introduce the concept of harmony and holding your part. There are many rounds in this book.

- Remember that the purpose in singing is not to produce concert sound but to facilitate participation, enjoyment and group harmony.

- After the sound and music have stopped, tune in to the silence, the underlying meditative state that is present at all times. This is your opportunity to absorb all the healing vibrations that have been created.

# The Power of Dance

Dance has been used throughout the ages by all cultures for healing, meditation and celebration. Movement is as natural to our lives as breathing. Like chanting, movement helps us to express our inner spirit through outer form, to ground and physcalize our intentions and inspirations. All peoples of the world have traditions of sacred/ folk dances. Some dances are done in circles on the earth; others in temples and churches. The movements may reflect nature or imitate animals; they are usually simple and repetitive.

## Working with Dances

### Dance Forms

There are three common dance forms used by groups: the circle, the chain/snake dance, and the spiral dance.

### The Sacred Circle

The symbol of the sacred circle is universal and has been used in rituals and ceremonies throughout time. Ancient stone circles, carvings and other archeological evidence have been found in the caves of our earliest ancestors. The circle is a powerful symbol of unity and wholeness connecting us with the cycles of life. The center of the circle is like the center of the universe. As we move around the circle, we learn to develop balance, and to find the relationship between our inner and outer lives. (For more on the Sacred Circle, see Chapter One, Creating Sacred Space.)

### 1. The Circle Dance

In this dance, participants move around a circle, generally side-stepping, and linking hands. When circle members face inward, the group energy is contained and a charge is built up easily. When they face outward, the group energy is sent out to others and to the planet for healing. The direction of the movement is important. The clockwise direction is solar and connects us with active, masculine *yang* energy. The counterclockwise direction is lunar and connects us with receptive, feminine *yin* energy. The solar direction helps to build a concentration of energy and draw in positive forces; the lunar direction diffuses and releases energy.

### 2. Chain/Line / Snake Dance

The line/snake dance is a variation of the circle. Dancers begin in a circle, but then one person (the leader) lets go of the hand of one of her/his neighbors so that the circle becomes a line, chain or snake. (For more on the power of the snake see Chapter Four—Woman Power, pp. 104–5.)

• The chain/snake of dancers can double or triple or more around so that people begin to pass each other face-to-face, making eye contact in their respective lines. The lines can weave in various patterns such as making concentric circles, forming a spiral, weaving in and out of each other; making bridges with partners while others go under them. The chain/snake can wind around the room, and separate into several snakes. All can face in one direction like a train as each dancer puts her or his hands on the shoulders or waists of the person in front of them. The snake can move fast and make many curves, creating a whip-like effect; or move more slowly, in a more focused way. You can also experiment with gradually building up power, speed and intensity, then returning to a slower pace.

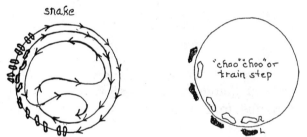
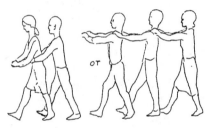

### The Sacred Spiral

The spiral pattern, inherent in the circle, is a very old, sacred symbol of initiation and personal power. It has been found on historic sites throughout the world. (One of the most famous, which extends over several miles, is in Nazca, Peru.) The spiral differs from the circle in that it never closes, but keeps expanding outward, forming ever-widening concentric circles. The spiral movement can go high up into the outer atmosphere or deep down into the earth, or both, spinning clockwise or counterclockwise. It has the potential to shift us from one dimension of reality to another, into limitless time and space, deep into the core of our being. The center of the spiral is the quiet stillpoint, the 'eye' at the center of the cyclone, where we experience the primal source of all possibilities.

### 3. The Spiral Dance

To create a spiral dance, follow the instructions for the chain/snake dance with all participants standing in a circle, holding hands.

• The leader lets go of the hand of one of their neighbors and leads the group in a slow chain dance, following a spiral pattern toward a center point.

· The energy builds in intensity as the chain spirals around. Each dancer holds a common focus, and directs their thoughts toward a desired goal. They can look into the eyes of others as they pass by to build group solidarity.

· When the leader reaches the center of the spiral, everyone moves in closer, raising their arms, chanting strongly to create a focal point of energy. This is known as " raising a cone of power." It is the moment when the accumulated power can be channelled for healing; when the desired individual/collective goals/prayers can come into manifestation.

Some spiral dances end in the center after the power has been raised. Other dances unwind the spiral: the last person in the chain leads the group back into one large circle, usually in silence. The original leader, in the center, is the last to move.

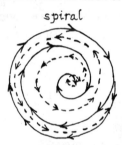

spiral

It's important when you have ended any of the dances to ground yourself well: lean over, touch your hands to the earth or stand in a balanced way feeling roots growing from your feet, connecting you deep into the earth.

## Dance Steps

Several simple steps can be used:

### The Side Step

The basic side-step is used in most circle dances. The sun, clockwise direction is described here, but the pattern can be reversed to be done moon, counterclockwise. Move L foot 12" (30cm), then on the next beat, bring the R foot to join the L. Continue this simple side-stepping pattern. The side step is usually done facing into the center of the circle but can also be done facing outward, especially when there is an inner and outer circle.

side step

L   R

**The Grandmother Step**

This step comes from the Native American tradition. It is a variation of the basic side step, (going clockwise) as described above. Move L foot 12" (30 cm) bend your L knee, sink into earth, and put all your weight on your L connecting with the magnetic energies of the Mother Earth. (This can also be done with a more active stamp) Then on the 'silent' beat, bring your R foot to meet the L, feeling an upward rising movement, connecting you to Father Sky and cosmic energies. Continue this pattern in the same direction. Alternate feeling one with Mother Earth as you sink down with your L foot, and one with Father Sky as you draw the R foot to meet the L. Your feet stamp on the down beat. As you do the grandmother step, feel your connection with everything around you–with 'all your relations'. Reverse the pattern going counter-clockwise. Do the step holding hands in a circle, or in a more expressive way leaving hands free to improvise, as in the African dances and *Blood of the Ancients* in Chapter Three.

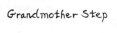 Grandmother Step

**Ghost dance step**

The following steps come out of the Native American Ghost Dance tradition and are more elaborate variations of side-stepping. The Ghost Dance was founded in the late 1880's by a Paiute Indian named Wovoka. Through a vision, he was given sacred songs and dances that would help his despairing people reunite and reclaim their spirit. The Ghost dance movement, although short–lived, raised the hope and consciousness of many .

**Version #1**—One step per beat. Side step to R (weight on R foot), bring L to meet R with a stamp. Then Side step L (weight on L foot) and bring R to meet L with a stamp. Continue this pattern, (Step R, Stamp L; Step L, Stamp R) advancing slowly around circle. This can be done in either direction. Combine with simple arm movements: Link arms and hands– raise them to shoulder level–making a W, and then lower them to hip level–making a V. (See arm diagram.)

**Version #2**—Lightly stamp L foot in place, then on next beat move it 12" (30 cm) to the L and stamp it again, simultaneously transferring your weight onto it. On next beat, stamp R foot where it is, then move it 12" to join the other foot, stamping and transferring weight onto it. Continue with this pattern. (Stamp L, Step L; Stamp R, Step R) advancing slowly around circle in either direction. Use the same arm movements.

### The Grapevine Step

This is another popular variation of the side-step used a lot in traditional folk dances of the Middle East and Europe. If you are moving to the right, put your L foot behind the R, step sideways with the R, then step in front of R foot with the L, step to side with R, etc. Continue this pattern as you link hands or shoulders. Reverse to go into the opposite direction.

Grapevine Step

### Spinning

Spinning activates the life force and stimulates your whole energy system. As you spin you are calling forth new life. Imagine something you want to manifest, and literally set it in motion as you turn. You are moving between the worlds into an altered state of consciousness, spinning within the sacred spiral. It is dangerous to spin for long periods (as do the whirling dervishes ) unless you have a lot of experience. Find a fixed point in your environment to focus on, keeping your eyes open. This helps you stay in balance and find the stillpoint at the center. Be aware of the different effects of spinning to the right or the left.

### Hand Positions

When moving in a circle, your hands are commonly held in a V or W position or around shoulders of neighbors.

**In a V**          **In a W**

V-hold          W-hold

### Mudras

You can distill your experience into a simple series of movement patterns which are repeated over and over like a mantra. These movement patterns, especially those done with the upper body, hands and fingers, are known in Sanskrit as 'mudras.' In the yogic traditions they are combined with different postures and breathing practices. Try using mudras in the following ways:

> • Choose one or two qualities, or divine attributes you would like to affirm and embody more fully. These can come from the words of one of the chants such as 'I am the dance of the moon and sun'.

(For an example see the Shiva mudra in Chapter Five.)

• Translate these qualities into a few simple mudra movements. Repeat them over and over. Try repeating them with and without accompanying words and sounds.

• As you repeat the movements, they become your meditation, your gestures of affirmation.

You can also intensify the power of a chant by moving and swaying your head and upper torso in rhythm with the beat.

## Guidelines for Sharing the Dances

• Make sure the group knows the chant/song well before you begin doing the movements as a group.

• If the movements are simple, begin to dance immediately. Describe and demonstrate as you go. The group will usually pick the steps up quickly. Don't talk too much; try to get people out of their heads and into their bodies as quickly as possible. If the dance is more complicated, involving partners, break it down into segments, demonstrating and practicing each part separately. After everyone has learned the dance, begin again. Encourage group attunement and fuller expression.

• When the chant/dance is a round, it is possible to dance in as many circles as there are parts. Each circle begins to move and chant when it is their turn to come in.

• When the dance requires changing partners, have the partners face each other within the circle and look ahead in the direction in which they are going. The next person they see facing them will be their next partner.

## Creating your own chants and dances

As you become more experienced with chanting and dancing, your own inspiration and creativity may begin to emerge. Here are a few suggestions for creating your own chants and dances :

• Begin with an already existing melody and rhythm and add your own words.

• Or begin with words and let melody and rhythm come forth. If the chant doesn't come easily, take more time to tune into the natural rhythm of the words. Play with it for a while, emphasizing different words and syllables. The melody can be very simple, just using one or two tones with which you are comfortable. Experiment till you have what you want. Don't judge. Trust what you first receive.

• Make sure that the words are uplifting in some way. For inspiration, you might choose a favorite prayer or poem, or spend time meditating in nature. Listen to the sounds of the wind, the flowing of a brook, the chirping of a bird or hear the voice of a tree or rock as you sit next to it. Begin to echo the natural sounds you hear. Join your song with the song of nature. Clap two sticks or stones together to provide rhythm.

· Many traditional people use medicine chants to heal themselves and others and get in touch with their power at different times in their life. Discover your own personal healing 'medicine' power chant: Listen deeply within yourself to the source of your inner power, to the voice of your own being. Chant over and over the appropriate words of power, healing or affirmation you need at this time such as, ' I will not be afraid. I have the courage of a bear.'

## Information and Resources

There are over three hundred songs and chants in this collection, gathered over many years from various retreats, workshops, and healing/ritual circles. Some have their roots in ancient religions and native traditions; others come out of the human potential, new age, neo-pagan/shamanic movements that have grown in America and Europe since the late 60's. Some have been created spontaneously by one or more people during prayer, meditation and ceremony. The women's spirituality movement has also been a rich source of chants. The majority are in the English language, but there are also chants and songs from many global sources including Native American, African, Celtic, Mayan, Maori, Aboriginal and Japanese. The accompanying dances, by Kate Marks, draw their inspiration from folk and sacred circle dance traditions.

As these chants and songs have been passed on mostly through an oral tradition, they have changed and evolved over time; many versions exist. It is not always possible to trace the original. It is also difficult to 'fix' them in book form. Great efforts have been made to trace sources, and receive permissions when possible. If any song, or chant has not been correctly notated or credited, please let us know.

Before leading the chants and dances, it is best to study directly with an experienced teacher for an extended period. Learning from a book such as this is not enough. For information and further resources, see the list in the appendix. A 90-minute audio tape called *Journeys in Sound and Healing* is also currently available, which discusses the healing power of vibration and sound and includes guided meditations and exercises to free the voice and restore health. Workshops and seminars on many of the themes in this book can be set up in your area.

If you have written or know of special chants, (especially from other cultures or from the men's movement) that can be included in future volumes, please send them with their meaning and sources, preferably sung on tape with accurate musical notation.

As we sing and dance, we join spiritually with others on the planet and lay the foundations for a peaceful harmonious world. We celebrate our unity and diversity, and honor all our spiritual paths. Our reverberation expands in spirals of light and sound, like the ripples of a pebble dropped in a pond.

## Let us open our hearts and spirits and join together in a circle of song!

# Chapter One

# Creating Sacred Space

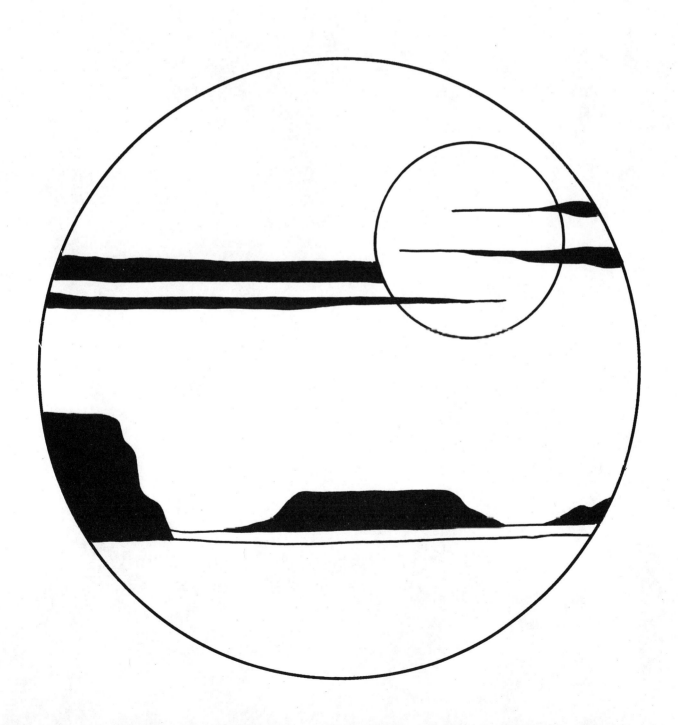

# Sacred Space

## Meditation—Creating Sacred Space

*Close your eyes and bring your focus within. Become aware of your breath as it flows in and out. Release any tensions and preoccupations. Imagine yourself in a sacred holy space, full of power and beauty. Look around you. What is this place like? What makes it holy and sacred for you? Experience the richness of each detail; the colors, sounds, smells, and textures. You may find you are in a peaceful natural landscape; or in the inner chamber of an ancient temple.*

*Take a moment to sit quietly in meditation, being open and receptive, listening for any messages or guidance you may receive. When you are ready open your eyes and return slowly.*

## Creating Sacred Space

Before you chant, dance or do ritual/ceremony, it is important to create a sacred space, a holy temple.

Physically—Choose a sacred environment that is quiet, uncluttered, conducive to meditation, where you will not be disturbed. Set up a simple altar, light a candle and incense. Lay out your favorite magical objects, such as crystals. If outdoors, seek a private spot in nature where you feel safe, empowered and inspired.

Mentally—Quiet your mind. Focus on your breath, letting all your thoughts go. Imagine yourself in a magical holy place. Visualize your inner temple with rich detail.

The following chants help to create sacred space:

# Temple Round

*Words: Hazrat Inayat Khan  Music: W.A. Mathieu*

Round in four parts (optional)

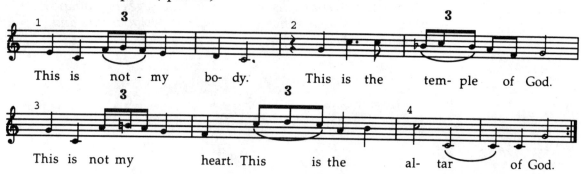

This is not-my bo-dy. This is the tem-ple of God.

This is not my heart. This is the al-tar of God.

# God of Beauty

For more simplicity, sing unaccompanied.

God of beau-ty is now dwel-ling in the tem-ple of my heart, of my

heart, of my heart of my heart of my heart.

# Where I Sit is Holy

*Native American*

Where I sit is ho- ly, ho- ly is this ground.

fo- rest, moun- tain, ri- ver lis- ten to the sound. Great spi- rit

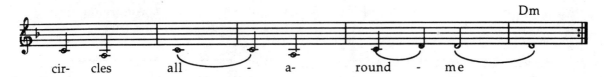

cir- cles all - a- round - me

**Verses:**

Add other verses such as 'Where I/we dance(pray,love,sing) is holy'

What I do is holy, holy is my way
Life and work together, celebrate the day (Barbara Clark)

Where we sing is holy,sacred is this place
as we breathe together, we fill with light and grace

# Now I Walk in Beauty

*Text: Hopi Prayer   Music: Gregg Smith*
*Recorded by Libana on The Fire Within*

Now I walk in beau- ty. Beau- ty is be- fore me,

Beau- ty is be- hind me, a- bove and be- low me.

**Dance:**
Walk sunwise in a circle.
**Now I walk in Beauty**—Arms out to side embracing all beauty.
**Beauty is before me**—Stretch arms in front of you.
**Beauty is behind me**—Twist your upper body and head
around,facing behind you as you stretch arms back behind you
**Above and below me**—Raise arms to sky, then to earth.

# Spirit is Around Us

*William Baker*
*Recorded on* Path of the Heart

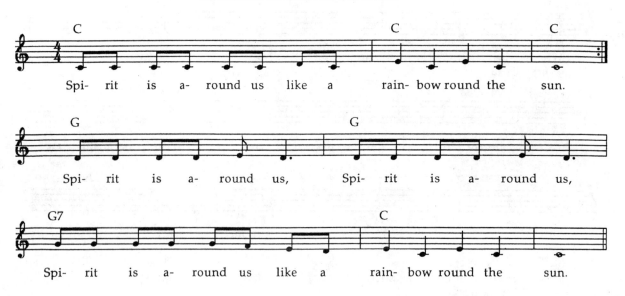

Spi- rit is a- round us like a rain- bow round the sun.

Spi- rit is a- round us, Spi- rit is a- round us,

Spi- rit is a- round us like a rain- bow round the sun.

Chant this for a long time making up your own verses. Substitute 'me' or 'you' or a particular name or quality as appropriate.

**Verses:**
Love is around us like a rainbow around the sun.
Put your arms around us like a rainbow around the sun.
Goddess is inside us like a river inside the earth.

# O Great Spirit

Oh, Great Spi - rit, Earth, Sun, Sky and Sea. You are in- side - and

all a- round - me.

**Verse:**

Oh Holy Mother,
Earth and moon and sea
You are inside
And all around me.

## Calling in Our Power

We all have sources of power and wisdom within us—helpers and guides who work with us in the spirit realms, whether we are aware of them or not. As we create sacred space, we can invite these spiritual forces to be with us for blessing, protection, guidance and inspiration. Our guides and teachers take many forms; they can appear as entities separate from us (such as animals, ancestors and angels) or as aspects of ourselves.

Through invocation, an active form of prayer, call on your sources of wisdom and power to join you in your sacred space.

### Meditation—Opening to Spiritual Power

*Go to or imagine yourself in a place of spiritual power, where you feel connected with your inner wisdom and sources of guidance. Explore this landscape of power. Look around you. See what images and symbols speak to you. Find a symbol or object which symbolizes your spiritual power. It may come to you as a brilliant sun or as a specific being or spirit guide. Take time to listen deeply and interact/dialogue with this image/object of power. Pose a question; ask for guidance and blessings. When you are done, give thanks for all you have received, express your gratitude to any helpers for being there with you and leave respectfully.*

# Power, Power, We Are Calling

Sing with drumbeat

Pow- er, pow- er we are call- ing. Pow- er, pow- er

we are call- ing. Come, come, be with us to- night!

As you sing, think about what powers or qualities you want to call in at this time to bring you strength, healing, protection and blessings.

**Verse:**
Change the words as appropriate. For example, 'Courage, courage', 'Peace, Peace', 'Joy, Joy', etc. Substitute 'I am calling' or 'Be with me/us now or today'. Call in the elements using the following phrases: Air, air, we are calling (2x), Come, come, **blow** it all away. Fire, Fire, we are calling (2x), Come come, **burn** it all away. Water, water,... **wash** it all away. Earth, earth,... **carry** it all away.

# Archangel Invocation

*Lisa Thiel*

*Recorded on* Songs of the Spirit © 1984

An invocation to the four Archangels: Michael corresponds to the South, fire, inner passion, the will and truth; Gabriel to the West, water, feelings, intuition and purity; Raphael to the East, air, clear thought and illumination; Uriel to the North, earth, wisdom and abundance.

An - gel - Mi - chael    An - gel - Gab - riel -    An - gel - Ra - pha - e -

l-    An-    gel- Au - ri el

**Verse:**
All the teachers of the light
Help us in our earthly plight
Open up our other sight
All the teachers of the light.

# Wani Wachialo—Wakan Tanka
*Native American Chant*

Sing with a strong, fast drumbeat or rattle shake.

Wa·ni   wa·chi·a·lo.   Wa·ni·wa··chi·a·lo.

Wa·kan ~ ka tan·ka.   Wa·kan ~ ka tan·ka.

This power chant invokes the creator, the Great Spirit and the life force. It means 'Thank you for this life, O Great Spirit'.

# We Are the Power in Everyone
*Starhawk*
*Additional verses by Lorelei*

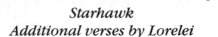

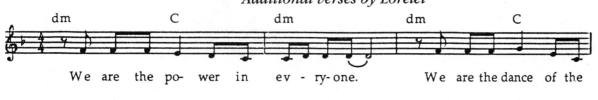

We are the po-wer in ev·ry·one.   We are the dance of the

moon and sun.   We are the hope that will   ne - ver hide.

We  are  the  tur-ning   of - the tide

**Verses:**
We are the spirit (love, growth) in everyone.
We are the dance of the rising (setting) sun.

# Hey Ungawa

*Native American Welcoming Song—Chumash Tradition.*

This chant honors the dawn and the four directions. The Chumash people sing it in their ceremonies to protect their land and ask for guidance and blessings. They rise before the sun, considered by the elders as a most auspicious time for prayer and contemplation, and chant to greet the sun's first rays, the dawning of a new day. They ask for Wisdom from the Spirits of each of the Four Directions.

Sing the entire chant to each Direction (first East, then South, West, North ) at sunrise, if possible. End the chant by saying Ho (So be it) three times, sending a blessing to the earth. Accompany with rattle only.

# Ungala We

*Australian Aboriginal Power Chant*

Sing fast and joyously, with steady drumbeat and a variety of simple percussion sticks and rattles, etc.

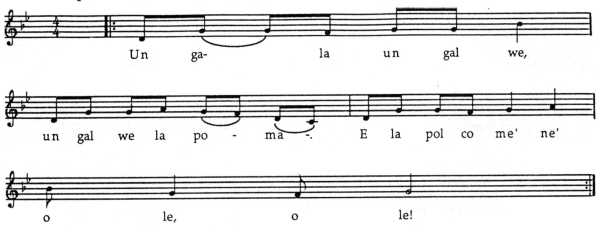

Un ga- la un gal we,

un gal we la po - ma -. E la pol co me' ne'

o le, o le!

Sing the Native words to start and end each verse. Make up your own words of affirmation for the English part. For example: 'I am a strong woman, I am a story woman, I am a healer, my soul will never die.'

**Verses**

I am a mother, I am a seeker

I am a teacher, my soul will never die

Ung a la un gal we un gal we la poma

E la polco me'ne ole' ole'

**Dance:**

In an outer circle, all do a side step, Grandmother, or Ghost dance step. In the center, each person takes a turn to freely express their dance of power and affirmation.

# Ib Aché (eeb ashay)

*African Spirit Welcoming Song*

Chant this as you face each of the four directions:

Ah - ib a che' ib a che' o ib ba ba ba ib ba ye ye

ib a ché

Translation:

Hail to the gifts

Hail to my own gifts

Hail to Father Sky

Hail to Mother Earth

Hail to the gifts!

11

# We are Alive

*Rose May Dance/Starhawk ©*
*Recorded on* Chants–Ritual Music, *Reclaiming Community.*

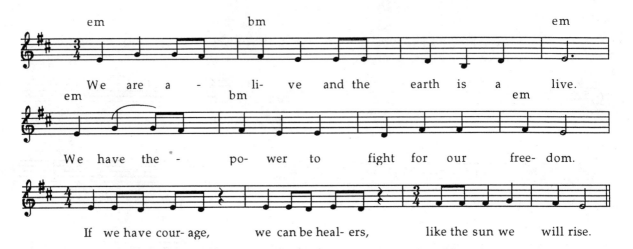

We are a- li- ve and the earth is a live.

We have the - po- wer to fight for our free- dom.

If we have cour- age, we can be heal- ers, like the sun we will rise.

**Verse:**

Substitute 'I' instead of 'we'. Also try 'Like the moon we shall rise.'

# Apache Power Chant

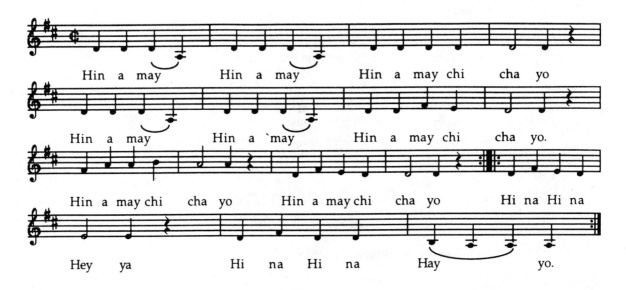

Hin a may Hin a may Hin a may chi cha yo

Hin a may Hin a 'may Hin a may chi cha yo.

Hin a may chi cha yo Hin a may chi cha yo Hi na Hi na

Hey ya Hi na Hi na Hay yo.

The following chants are used to call in our spiritual power; to help us seek, remember and understand our visions and dreams. It is during periods of meditation, retreat and intense purification that we are most open and receptive.

In many Native American traditions, a vision quest ceremony is performed. This is a ceremony of initiation, often done as part of a rite of passage from one life stage to another. The vision questers go out alone in the wilderness for several nights without food or drink and sit in meditation seeking guidance, power and visions about their life path. They return deeply transformed to share their experiences and visions with their elder guides and communities. Many people today, of all ages and colors, are adopting the vision quest ceremony.

# Holy Vision

*Words: Taken from Native American Pawnee Ceremony*
*Music: Michael Tierra*

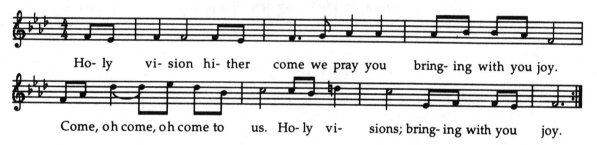

Ho- ly   vi- sion hi- ther   come we pray you   bring- ing with you joy.

Come, oh come, oh come to   us. Ho- ly vi- sions; bring- ing with you   joy.

**Verse:**
Holy vision here they are approaching to us
here bringing them with joy.
Nearer still they come, holy visions,
holy visions; bringing with them joy.

Holy visions; go before the door, where they pause, waiting.
Bearing gifts of joy, pausing as they wait.
Holy visions, bearing gifts of joy.

# Behold a Sacred Voice

*Words: Black Elk (from Black Elk Speaks) Music: Marlena Fontenay*

Be- hold, be- hold. A sa- cred voice is cal- ling us. Be-

hold, be- hold. All o- ver the sky, a sa- cred voice is

cal- ling us. Be- hold, be- hold.

Sing it through all the way, or sing any of the lines separately over and over like a mantra, improvising and weaving beautiful harmonies. It can also be done as a round.

# Dreamtime

*Osha Drury*
*Recorded on* Eye of the Aeon © *Silver on the Tree*, 1990

Dream time, Dream- time. Wake up to the Dream- time

Keep your feet on the ground and your head in the stars Dance your dream a- wake.

Keep your feet on the ground and your head in the stars

Dance your dream a- wake. Dream your dance a- wake

A chant inspired by the Australian Aboriginal people who, for over 40,000 years, have understood the power of visions and dreams; what they call 'the dreamtime'.

The following power dance can be done with any power chant. It is best to have another person drumming who follows the dancer's feet.

## Power Dance

*Stand in a sacred circle and ground yourself well. Imagine you have roots going from the bottoms of your feet deep into the core of the earth.*

*Begin to actively call in your power. Lift your feet slightly off the ground one at a time in rhythm with the drum, feeling the gravitational pull of the earth.*

*Dance as if you are pulling your power up under your feet. Feel each beat of the drum deepening your connection with your source of power.*

*Focus on your breath and synchronize your breathing with the pulse of the drum and the rhythm of the chant.*

*Improvise and move any way that feels right for you, affirming your personal power. You may want to imagine yourself transforming into a specific animal.*

*Let your power dance slowly build and reach a peak and then gradually subside, coming to a place of inner stillness.*

## The Sacred Circle
### Honoring the Four Directions

The symbol of the sacred circle is universal. (See the introduction) Also known as a mandala or medicine wheel, the sacred circle connects us with the cycles of life; with feelings of unity and wholeness. It represents our soul's journey from birth to death to rebirth. Within the circle is the square, the power of four which is also considered very sacred. For example: there are four directions, four seasons, four elements, four kingdoms (mineral, vegetable, animal, human), four races (black, yellow, red and white) to name but a few correspondences.

According to ancient wisdom, in order to become whole, we must experience all four quarters of the sacred circle and learn to integrate and harmonize these aspects within ourselves. In each of the four directions, specific powers and teachings are given to us. The associations given to the directions vary from tradition to tradition. The four directions are often associated with the four elements, the seasons, the cycles of the sun as well as other attributes such as colors, animal totems, etc. One popular system makes the following correspondences: East is associated with air, spring, the sunrise and the intellect; South with fire, spirit, summer and midday; West with water, autumn, sunset and the emotions; and North with earth, the body, winter, and midnight. Often, the directions of the Sky (above), the Earth (below) and the sacred Center, the place within, are also invoked.

Find what feels right for you. Take time to explore for yourself and discover your own symbols and associations as you move around the sacred circle.

## Sacred Circle Meditation

*Create a sacred circle. Make the circle large enough for you to stand in and walk a few feet in each direction.*

*Stand in the center of your circle in whatever direction feels right. Become aware of the energy, the vibrations at this sacred Center, the place Within. Experience yourself coming into perfect alignment with heaven and earth and all the universal forces.*

*Honor the Above, the spirit of Father Sky by reaching your arms upward.*

*Honor the Below, the spirit of Mother Earth by kneeling down and touching the earth.*

*Begin to turn slowly in the center, moving sunwise, experiencing each of the directions.*

*Face to the East stretching arms and hands out in front of you. Take some time to experience and honor the energy of this direction.*

*Then continue around the circle, honoring each of the directions in a similar way.*

*When you have completed the circle, take a moment to thank each of the directions and all the forces you have encountered.*

# A Circle is Cast

*Anna Dembska ©*
*Recorded by Libana on* A Circle is Cast *© 1986*

    This chant helps us to create (cast) a sacred circle. Sing it as a three part round over a drone line, moving toward the ending coda, which is chanted in four parts till the energy peaks. Then slow the chant back down and ground by touching the earth.

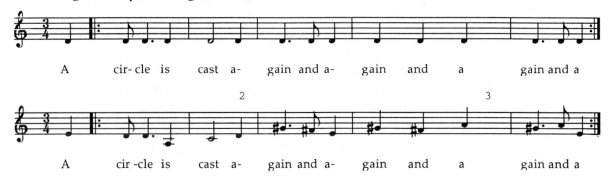

**The Coda:**

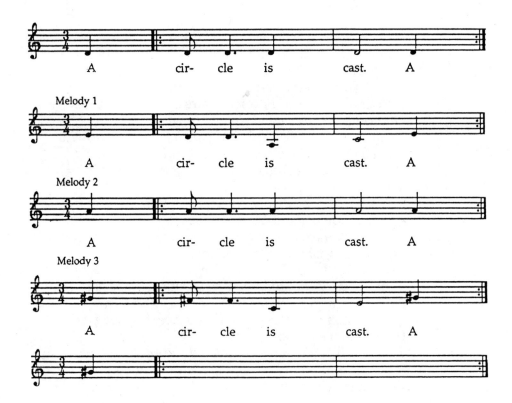

As you call on the power of each direction, say a simple prayer and invocation. Call on the powers of God and Goddess, Christ, your ancestors, spirit guides, teachers, or anything else you wish to have bless, protect, and inspire you. Say something like 'I ask that all of our masters, teachers, angels, and guides be with me/us, to bless, inspire and protect me/us,' or 'I call for the powers of healing and transformation to be with me/us for the highest good of all.' Place sacred objects such as representations of the four elements on your altar, and call out the names of different things that are meaningful and empowering for you. Be open to the spirit of guidance and protection in your life. Create ways to invite these forces into your sacred space. The most powerful times to do invocations are the new and full moons, the equinoxes and solstices, as well as special holidays.

When you have finished with your sacred work, say a few sentences to release all the energies you have invoked and thank them for assisting you.

# Invocation to the Four Directions
*Kate Marks*

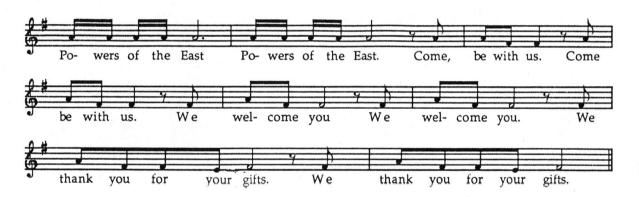

Do as a call and response: repeat each line a second time as response.

　　　　Powers of the East, (repeat as response)——————
Spirit of the Air,——"——————
　　　　Come be with us——"——————
　　　　We welcome you——"——————

To thank the powers at the end of your ceremony change third and fourth lines to:

　　　　We wish you well
　　　　We thank you for your gifts.

Add different qualities for each direction, for example.' Power of the Eagle, Spirit of the winged ones.' Continue this for each direction, using appropriate simple movements.

# Song to the Four Directions

*Peter and Harriet Calhoun*

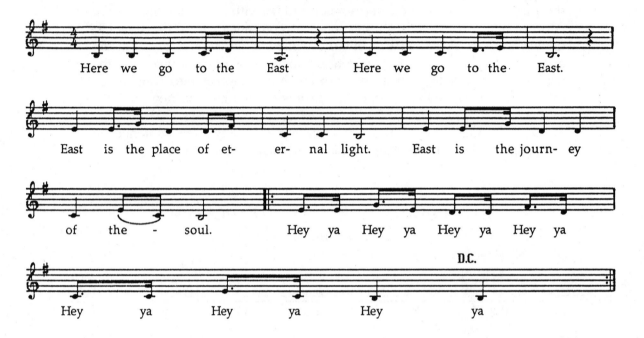

Here we go to the East  Here we go to the East.

East is the place of et- er- nal light.  East is the journ- ey

of the - soul.  Hey ya Hey ya Hey ya Hey ya

**D.C.**

Hey ya Hey ya Hey ya

**Verses:**

South is the place of the eternal flame.
West is the place of the healing waters.
North is the place of eternal darkness.

**Sioux Prayer**

*O, our Father the Sky, hear us and make us strong.*
*O, our Mother the Earth, hear us and give us support.*
*O, Spirit of the East, send us your Wisdom.*
*O, Spirit of the South, may we tread your path of life.*
*O, Spirit of the West, may we always be ready for the long*
  *journey.*
*O, Spirit of the North, purify us with your cleansing winds.*

# Call to Spirit – Invocation Song

This was learned at the 1985 Pagan Spirit Gathering from Anodea Judith and Selene Vega.

Spi- rits of the------------` we're cal- ling- you

Spi- rits of the ---------- we're cal- ling you here  Spi- rits of the ----, we' re cal-

ling you here and  now  Spi- rits of the air,  bring your bles- sings fair;

Spi- rits of the sky, teach  us how to fly;  Spir-its of the East  in - to our Cir- cle

come.

Spirits of the Fire, bring us our desire;  Spirits of the ocean, deepen our emotion;
Spirits of the flame, burn away the pain;  Spirits of the sea, let the soul be free;
Spirits of the South into our Circle come!  Spirits of the West, into our Circle come!

Spirits of the land, help us understand;
Spirits of the earth, bring to us re-birth;
Spirits of the North, into our circle come!

# Spirit Invocation

Spi- rits of  the East:  Spi-rits of the South;  Spi- rits of the West;

Spi-rits of the North;  Be  in  our  cir- cle  now.

# Four Winds Blessing

*From the Blue Star Album,* 'Moon Hooves in the Sand' *and the*
*Dragonfest Songbook, 1987.*

O     East     wind be be-     hind you,     calm     winds that     blow

Scent- ing the air a-     bove you; in     youth,     my heart     may     grow.

**Chorus**

E- ver it be re-     mem- bered.     E- ver it be re-     mem-     bered.

Ev- er it be re-     mem- bered and     guide you where you     may     go.

O, South wind be behind you
Warm wind that blows
Fire of love upon you
In passion my heart may grow.
**Chorus**
O, West wind be behind you
Stormy wind that blows
Waters of life remind you
In wonder my heart may grow.
**Chorus**
O, North wind be behind you
Ancient wind that blows
The greenwood be about you
In wisdom my heart may grow.
**Chorus**
O, four winds be behind you
Strong winds that blow
The lady's blessing upon you
In love my heart may grow.
**Chorus**

# Chapter Two

# The Elements

# The Elements

## Meditation—Invocation to the Elements

*Spirit of Air, power of the four winds, of the winged ones, grant me the gift of clarity and vision.*

*Spirit of Fire, power of the sun, of the burning flame, grant me the gift of passion and vitality.*

*Spirit of Water, power of the oceans, and running streams, grant me the gift of deep feelings and conscious dreams.*

*Spirit of Earth, power of the trees and majestic mountains, grant me the gift of abundance and strong roots.*

# The Four Elements

Most spiritual traditions work with the four elements—earth, water, fire and air. These energies are present in all things. They are the foundation of life. Each element has unique healing and cleansing properties that we need in order to come into balance. Each element represents a different aspect of our being. Air represents the mind; fire—the spirit, water—the emotions; earth—the body. As you create a sacred circle, explore the meaning each element has for you. Place an object which represents each of the four elements on an altar. For example—use a candle for fire, a feather or incense for air, a bowl or chalice for water, a special crystal or stone for earth.

## Power of the EARTH

The Earth element is associated with our bodies. It helps us to connect with our physical nature, and be at home on the planet. It relates to issues of our survival, security, abundance, and our ability to manifest that which we envision and dream. Energetically, it is centered in the area from our feet up through our legs to the base of the spine (coccyx). The physical sense associated with the earth is touch. When earth energy is out of balance we are not grounded, we have deep fears of letting go, of moving forward in our lives. We become rigid, overly material, afraid of change.

### Mother Gaia Meditation

*Stand in a powerful place in nature. Imagine you have roots growing from the bottoms of your feet. Feel the vibration and magnetism of the earth flowing through you, up through your feet. Visualize yourself becoming very small and taking a journey down through your roots, deep into the center, the fiery core of the earth. As your eyes become accustomed to the light, look around you. Notice all the details of this inner earth landscape.*

*Gradually become aware of the presence of the Earth Mother Gaia standing near you. Study her form, her face. Look deep into her eyes. Feel her love and compassion as well as her pain and suffering. Interact with her; listen to her story. Ask her what she needs from you. Receive her guidance, her blessings and gifts.*

*Let your heartbeat join with her heartbeat as you chant her name—GAIA, GAIA over and over. Send her healing energy, surrounding her with light and love. When you are ready, give thanks and bid her farewell, knowing you can return at any time. Slowly begin your journey back the way you came and gently open your eyes.*

# The Earth is Our Mother
*Native American*

The Earth - is our mo - ther,

we must take care of her; the Earth - is our mo- ther,

we must take care of her; hey - yun- ga ho - yun- ga

hey - yung yung, hey - yun- ga ho - yun- ga

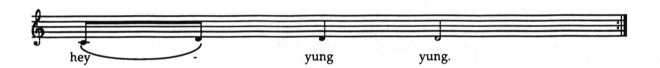

hey - yung yung.

**Verses:**
2. Her sacred ground we walk upon with every step we take.
3. The earth is our mother, she will take care of us.
4. The sky is our father, we will take care of him.
5. The sea is our sister, we will take care of her.
6. The forest is our brother etc.

**Dance:**

**The earth is our Mother etc.** Move around a circle doing the Side-step, Grandmother or Ghost dance steps (see Introduction). Be conscious of walking lightly on the earth. Hands are free, palms facing down drawing in earth energy. (For the verse about the sky, raise arms / hands heavenward, improvise for the others).

**Hey yunga, Ho yunga Hey yung yung:** Continue the same step as you make a full turn clockwise in place. Keep hands in same position, drawing in earth energy.

**Hey yunga, Ho yunga, Hey yung yung:** Facing into circle, side-step in place. Raise arms to Father Sky on 1st phrase; to Earth Mother on 2nd; and cross them over your heart on 3rd.

# Turn to the Mountain

*Joy Chappell ©*

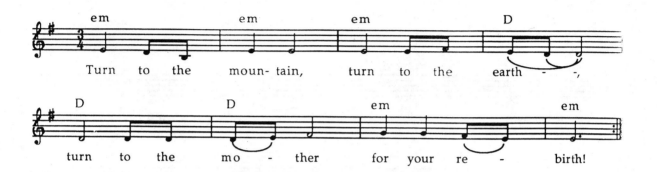

Turn to the moun- tain, turn to the earth -,
turn to the mo - ther for your re - birth!

Try chanting only the first verse, substituting different words such as 'Turn to the Goddess, turn to the earth', etc. Also each line can be sung twice, as a call and response.

**Verses:**

Mountain is calling
Children of light
Mother is calling
Come home to the light

Children are coming
From the ends of the earth
Children are coming
For their rebirth.

Land of the water
Land of the sun
Land of the sky
Home of the one

We are the children
the children of light
We are the children
We are the light.

We are the children
We are the light
We are the children
We are the light.

# We Are One With the Soul of the Earth

*Andreas Corbin Arthen © 1981, EarthSpirit Community*
Recorded on *All Beings of the Earth*

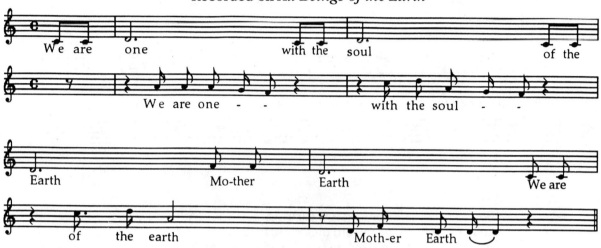

Sing for a long time. Improvise the second part and add harmonies.

# Terre Rouge

A traditional French country song that honors the red earth found in many sacred lands.

Translation: Red Earth, Earth of Fire, Earth of Light.
Red Earth under the Blue Sky.

The following two chants reflect the earth's perpetual motion and the continual cycles of life.

# Round and Round

*Recorded by Libana on* A Circle is Cast © 1986

Round and round the ea-rth is turn-ing, turn-ing al-ways ro-und to morn-ing, and from morn-ing ro-und to night.

**Dance:**

**Round and round the earth is turning**
Stand in a circle facing toward the center holding hands.
Take four side steps clock (sun) wise, beginning with left foot.

**Turning always round to morning**
Release hands. Spin individually in a clockwise direction making a slow full turn in place. Open arms from the heart and raise them above head slowly honoring the rising sun and the coming of day.

**And from morning round to night**
Continue turning individually in a clockwise direction as described above but now bring the head down and arms back to the heart, contracting with the coming of night.

# See the Earth is Turning

*Adele Getty*

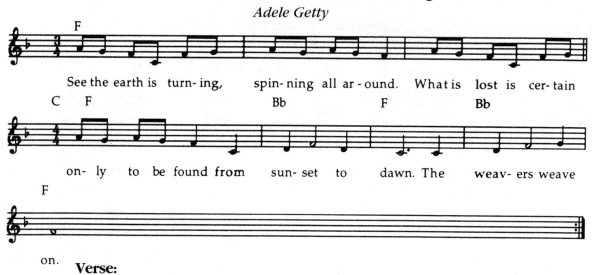

See the earth is turn-ing, spin-ning all ar-ound. What is lost is cer-tain on-ly to be found from sun-set to dawn. The weav-ers weave on.

**Verse:**

In the light of day our reason does abound.
But in the dark of night, we dream our way around.
From sunset to dawn, the weavers weave on.

## Power of the WATER

The water element is associated with the emotions, the feminine principle, the life force, purification, birth and regeneration. It influences the moon and tides, and connects us with our sexuality, intuition, and the unconscious aspects of our being. Energetically, it is centered in our reproductive organs, in the pelvis, the basin of life. The water center (chakra) is found in our bodies between the ovaries in women and at the sacrum in men. The physical sense associated with it is taste. Imbalanced water energy can manifest as becoming too emotional, losing one's boundaries, taking on other people's feelings and becoming obsessed with relationships.

### Water Meditation

*Sit by your favorite body of water at a special time of day. Look deep into the water. Allow an image to emerge that represents the spirit, the essence of the water. Perhaps a female form, a water Goddess, comes to you. Open yourself to her teachings and guidance*

*As you gaze into the water, allow any thoughts, memories, and feelings to come up, to flow through you. Gently release any anger, pain or sadness you may be holding into the water. Give them to the Water Goddess. Then ask her for purification. Bathe in her clear waters. Feel her healing power as she cleanses and revivifies your body and soul.*

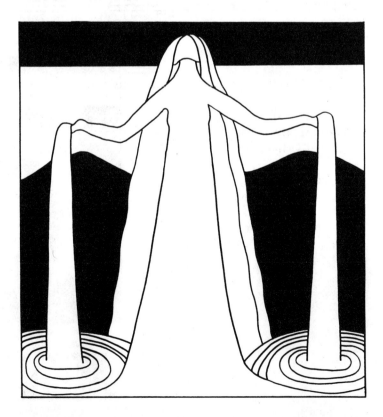

31

# The Ocean is the Beginning of the Earth

*Delaney Johnson/Starhawk*
*Recorded on* Chants—Ritual Music, *The Reclaiming Community*

Sing each part as a counterpoint.

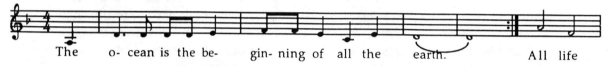

The o- cean is the be- gin- ning of all the earth. All life

comes from the sea

# Ocean Mother

*Innana Arthen, Earthspirit Community*
*Recorded on* All Beings of the Earth © 1990

Sing each part as a counterpoint.

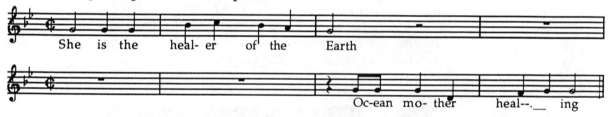

She is the heal- er of the Earth

Oc-ean mo- ther heal--.__ ing

**Verses:**
Ocean mother crying
She is the mourner of the Earth.

Ocean mother laughing
She is the brightness of the Earth.

Ocean mother birthing
She is the cradle of the Earth.

# Wichitai Tai

*Native American Chant*

Wi- chi  tai  ta  ti mu rai  hu- ra-ni- ka hu- ra-ni- ka  hey ne hey ne

no                                    a

The words means 'Water spirits are running round my head. I'm so glad I'm alive! '

# Born of Water

*Recorded on* Chants—Ritual Music, *The Reclaiming Community*

Round

Born  of  wa- ter,    clean-sing,  pow-er- ful,  heal- ing, chang-ing,

we                              are!

# Modok Chant

*Native American—Modok Tradition.*

Round

Hey  le  yo  chi  wee  yo  hey  le  yo

-.  Hey  Hey le  me  la  chi  way  ee  yo. Hey le

me  la  chi  wey  ee  yo.  Hey  le

This chant honors the water spirits. Sing each part twice.

# Ganga Ki Jai Jai

This traditional Hindu chant honors the sacred Ganges and Jamna rivers in India. Pilgrims travel long distances to receive blessings from these waters. 'Hail to the holy Ganges and Jamna rivers and hail to the sacred mountain Kailash, the earthly abode of Shiva.'

Jam- na    ki   Jai - Jai    Gan- ga   Ki   Jai   Jai

Kai- lash - pa- ti   Shi- va   Shan- kar  ki    Jai Jai

**Dance:**
Create a chain of dancers, holding hand. Weave in and out like two rivers.

# The River is Flowing

This chant describes beautifully the flow of life as a river, as it grows towards universal oneness. It invokes the spirit of water and of the Mother, and can connect us to our deep emotional life.

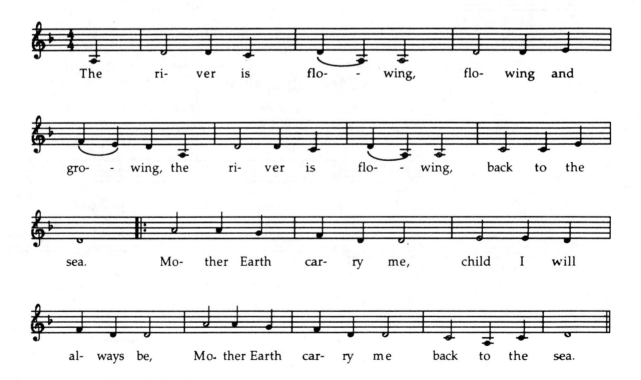

The    ri- ver   is   flo- - wing,    flo- wing  and

gro- - wing, the   ri- ver   is   flo- - wing,   back  to  the

sea.    Mo- ther Earth  car- ry  me,    child   I   will

al- ways  be,    Mo- ther Earth  car- ry  me   back   to   the   sea.

**Dance:**
1. The river
2. Is flowing
3. Flowing and growing
4. The river
5. Is flowing
6. Down to the sea

**Part 1**

1-6 Do the grapevine step in a circle, holding hands, moving counterclockwise.

Meditate on your life as a river, on what you are weaving behind you and then weaving in front of you.

**Part 2**

**7. Moth-er carry me**

All move into center of circle raising arms, calling to the Mother.

**8. Your child I will always be**

Move back out, bringing arms over chest making a cradle and rocking a baby in your arms.

**9. Moth-er carry me**

Same as # 7.

**10. Back to the sea or Carry me home.**

Move back out, opening arms back, receiving the sea.

**Verse 2**—Sing this version to honor sister moon and to open to the feminine spirit. This verse can be done separately or as part of the above.

**11. The moon she is waiting**

Side-step to R (moonwise), arms making a full circle above head (holding the moon).

**12. Waxing and waning**

Continue side-step R, cross arms/hands down over face, symbolizing the crescents of the moon.

**13. The moon she is waiting**

Same as # 11.

**14. Until we are free**

Spin in place, opening arms out.

**15. Sister moon watch over me**
**16. Your child I will always be**
**17. Sister moon watch over me**

#15–17; Same as # 7–9 above

**18. Until we are free**

Spin out from center of circle, arms outstretched.

This chant is also translated into Spanish:
El rio se va siendo
Dabdo creciendo
El rio se va siendo
hasta la mar.
Madre llevame,
nino siempre yo sere.
Madre llevame,
nino siempre yo sere.

## Power of the FIRE

The fire element is associated with spirit, passion, power, the male principle and transformation. It symbolizes light, our illumination, the divinity of the soul. It relates to the will, to our ability to be direct, active and assertive. Energetically, fire is connected to the solar plexus chakra, our digestive processes and the physical sense of sight. Imbalanced fire energy can lead to eruptions of anger, rage, fever and infection, or if deficient, fire leads to a loss of vitality and inner passion. Fiery people often burn out, over-extending themselves beyond their limits.

### Fire Meditation

*Meditate, chant and drum by an open fire in a sacred circle. Dance with the swirling flames and glowing colors. Feel the fire moving within you, warming and enlivening your spirit. Ask the fire spirits to reveal their inner nature; listen to their message and guidance for you.*

*As you hold a log or stick, get in touch with what you want to let go of, to change in your life. Fill the wood with those things you wish to release. When you are ready, throw it into the fire to be consumed and transformed.*

# Step into the Holy Fire

*Sanyassin Chant—Osho ( Rajneesh ) Community*

Step in- to the Ho- ly    fi - re;    step in- to the ho- ly fl- ame.

Ah -    -    -    -    - Alle -    lu-    ya.

As you chant, imagine yourself becoming one with the fire, and dancing in the flames. Try doing harmonies a third and fifth above the melody.

# Fire Flow Free

*Ariana Lighteningstorm*
*Recorded  on* Renewal *by* Kiva © 1991

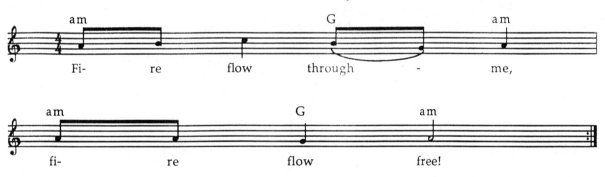

Fi-    re    flow    through    -    me,

fi-    re    flow    free!

# Rise With the Fire

*Starhawk* ©
*Recorded on* Chant—Ritual Music, *Reclaiming Community.*

We can rise with the fire of free-dom - - Truth is the fi- re that will burn our chains; we can stop the fi- re of des truc- tion - - Heal- ing is the fi-re run- ning through our veins, we can

# Firechild

*Thunderbird Woman*
*Recorded on* The Dawning—Chants of the Medicine Wheel

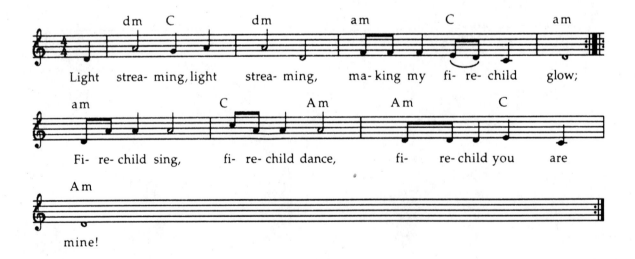

Light strea- ming, light strea- ming, ma-king my fi- re- child glow; Fi- re-child sing, fi- re-child dance, fi- re-child you are mine!

# Rise Up O Flame

*Christophe Praetorius*

Round: Sing in eight parts beginning at each measure.

Rise up, O flame by thy light glow-ing

Show to us beau- ty wis- dom - and joy

# Hotaru Koi

*Traditional Japanese*
*Recorded on* The Fire Within *by Libana,* 1990

Ho, ho, ho- ta- ru koi At - chi no mi- zu wa

ni- ga- i zo, Kot - chi no mi- zu wa a- ma- i zo,

Ho, ho, ho- ta- ru- koi.

This chant honors the firefly. It translates as 'Come firefly come. Over there the water is nasty. Over here the water is sweet.' Chant it as a round, imagining yourself in a field full of fireflies.

# Fire of the Heart

*Mary Ann Fusco*
*Recorded on* Aradia' s Songs for All Seasons © 1984

**Verses**

| | |
|---|---|
| Fire like a sword, | Fire in the sky, |
| fire like a shield, | fire in the sea, |
| fire to the core, | fire deep inside, |
| fire to be healed. | deep inside of me. |

## Power of the Sun

The following chants invoke the sun, associated with the fire element. The sun is the life force that sustains all life on earth. It helps us mark our passage from day into night, season into season, light into dark. Human beings have worshipped the sun from the beginning of time, especially at the Solstices and Equinoxes.

### Sun Meditation

*At sunrise, sit facing the sun. Meditate on light, on the dawning of a new day. Ask yourself what it is you wish to bring into your life. Thank the sun for illuminating your path.*

*At sunset, watch the sun as it disappears over the horizon. Reflect on your day and the coming darkness. What shadow aspects of your being do you need to confront? What do you want to release, or complete in your life? What do you need to work on in your night dreams?*

*Give thanks and make an offering to Father Sun; receive his blessings and gifts.*

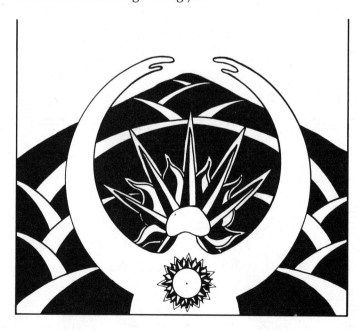

# Zuni Sunrise Song

*Recorded on* Medicine Wheel, *Spring Hill Music,* 1992

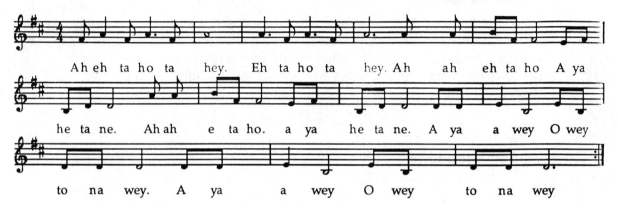

Ah eh ta ho ta hey. Eh ta ho ta hey. Ah ah eh ta ho A ya

he ta ne. Ah ah e ta ho. a ya he ta ne. A ya a wey O wey

to na wey. A ya a wey O wey to na wey

**English Verse:**
Ah eh ! Arise ! Arise!
Rise! Arise! Arise!
Ah eh Wake Up!
Life is calling you.
Ah eh Wake up!
Life is greeting you.
Father sun God, he is calling you.
Father sun God, he is greeting you.

Face the rising sun as you chant, arms raised in greeting.

# Cree Sunrise Song

*Recorded on Native American Ceremonial Chants*

This is sung by the village crier at sunrise. It means 'The birds are singing, something wonderful is coming'.

Sa sa pi a si sa ni kom a wah deb yo na se

hey ya kuan ka te ski na ya ha ya ha ha ya ha ya ha ha ha ya ha ya

ha ha ya ha ya ha ha ha ya

# Kuate Leno Leno

*Native American Chant   (English words by Robert Greenway )*

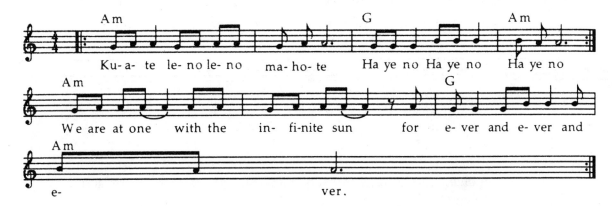

This is a chant to invoke the sun, the light, the father. Do it at sunrise or sunset. Use a strong fire drumbeat: four beats with emphasis on the first downbeat of each measure. The native words are pronounced Ku -Ha—Tay, Lay No, Ma—ho—tay.

# The Sun Goes Up

A simple sun chant, especially good for young children.

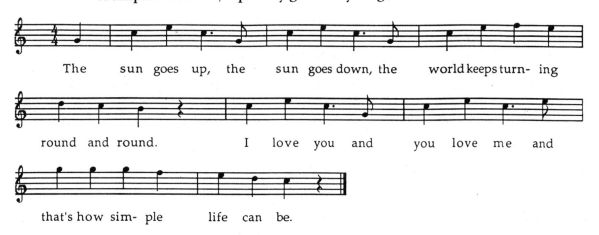

# Come, Children, Come to
# the Radiant Sun

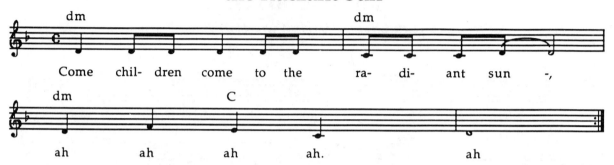

This sun chant can be used in many ways. Alter the words slightly and create your own movements.

**Verse Variations:**
Come O come to the radiant sun
I am (we are) one with the radiant sun.
For moon ceremonies, adapt the words:
I am (we are) in tune with the healing (power) of the moon
Ah Ah Ah Ah Ah

**Dance:**
Face the sun with your feet well grounded. Stand alone, or move slowly with others, sunwise in a circle, or in a line toward the sun.
**1. I am one with the radiant sun**
Hold hands at solar plexus. Imagine the sun radiating into this center. After singing the phrase, inhale deeply and hold your breath, feeling inner fire circulating through your whole being.
**2. Ah Ah Ah Ah Ah**
Exhale deeply, open hands outward to the sun. Expand the light out into the world.
3. Repeat # 1 and 2 with hands opening out from the heart.
4. Repeat # 1 and 2 with hands opening out from third eye (middle of forehead).

# Burning Fire Lights the Sun

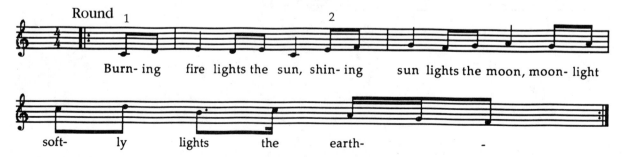

# Woke Up This Morning

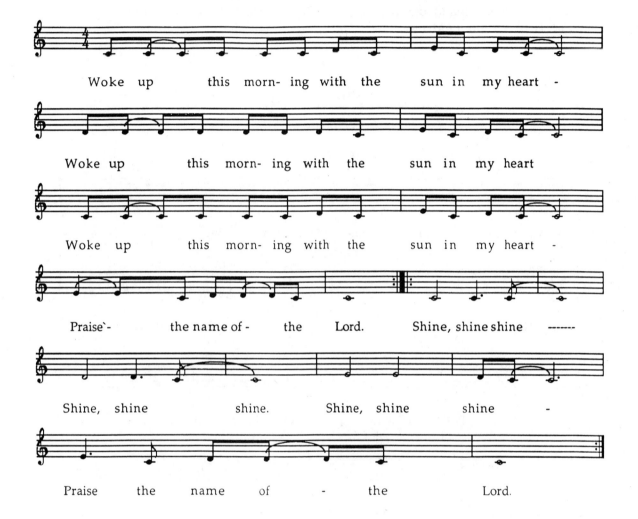

Woke up this morn- ing with the sun in my heart -

Woke up this morn- ing with the sun in my heart

Woke up this morn- ing with the sun in my heart -

Praise`- the name of - the Lord. Shine, shine shine -------

Shine, shine shine. Shine, shine shine -

Praise the name of - the Lord.

**Verse:**
(Substitute for Praise the name of the Lord)
1) I'll be shining all day
2) I'll be singing all day

### The Power of Light

The next chants invoke the power of light. They help us to experience and share our inner radiance.

# Pure White Light

*David Casselman* © 1981

Pu- re white light in the morn - ing, pu- re white light in the eve - ing too. Pu- re white light come sur- ro- und me. Pu- re white light keep shi - ning throught. Who can I be, who can I be? What do I see, what do I see?

# Be a Living Light

*Recorded on* Heartsongs by *Lia Argo*

Round

Be a li- ving light, take a

lit- tle bit and pass it on - high- er and

high- er and high- er. Light and - sound.

high- er and high - er. Lift up your voice in -

song

# This Little Light

This lit- tle light of mine I'm going to let it shine.

This lit- tle light of mine, I'm going to let it shine.

This lit- tle light of mine, I'm go -ing to let it shine, let it

shine, let it shine, let it shine.

# Light is Returning

*Charlie Murphy*
*Recorded on* Canticles of Light © 1984

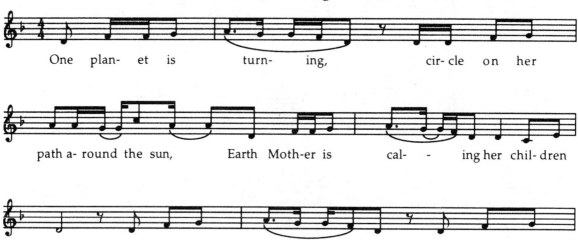

One plan- et is turn- ing, cir- cle on her

path a- round the sun, Earth Moth-er is cal - ing her chil- dren

home. Light is re- turn - ing al- though this

is the dark- est hour, no one can hold - back the dawn.

This chant is a powerful call to return to the light after times of darkness. It is particularly effective for a winter solstice gathering.

**Dance:**

**Verse #1**

**One planet is turning**

Form a circle. All face center and slowly side-step sunwise, arms in W, palms touching neighbor's palms.

**circle on her path around the sun**

Each person spins individually, sunwise, arms out.

**Earth mother is calling**

All go in toward the center, lifting arms and head slowly and holding them upward at center, calling to the mother.

**her children home.**

All move back out of center, lowering arms and sending energy into the earth.

**Verse #2**

Stand in place, facing into the center of the circle.

**Light is returning,**

Draw energy up from the earth. Place your hands together in a prayer position. Bring them past the heart to a point above the head; this symbolizes the inner flame.

**even though this is the darkest hour.**

Keep hands (in prayer position) above head. Visualize light burning through the darkest hours.

**No one can hold back the dawn.**
From the point above your head, slowly open arms to the sides,
greeting the dawn, the light.
**Verse #3**
All face in one direction; walk slowly clockwise.
**Let's keep it burning**
Walk as if holding a flame at heart level in front of you.
**Let's keep this fire of love (hope) alive**
Open hands out in front of you from the heart, invoking love/hope.
**Make safe the journey**
Circle slowly in place for a whole turn, returning to face center,
holding hands out as above.
**Through the storm.**
Face center, cross hands in front of you and then bring arms
down to sides.
Begin again from the first verse

# The Dawning of a New Day
*Traditional*
*Recorded on* The Dawning—Chants of the Medicine Wheel

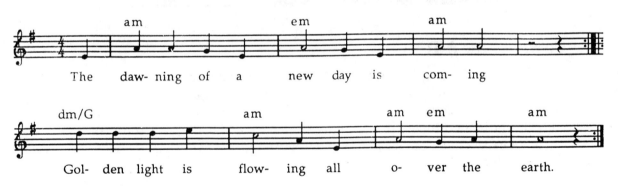

This chant can be used to celebrate the return of the light at the winter
solstice. It also invokes the New Age coming to earth, the awakening of our
consciousness.

## Power of the AIR

Air corresponds to our breath and life force; to the power of the mind, our intuition and intellect. It facilitates communication, spaciousness, movement, speed; the ability to cut through and think clearly. Air is associated with the heart and lungs, the nervous system, and the physical sense of smell. An excess of air can make us spacey, scattered and overly analytical.

### Air Meditation

*Stand on a mountain top. Enjoy the soft air and gentle breeze caressing your face. Listen to the whistling song of the wind, echoing through you. Watch the winged ones as they swoop and dance in the spacious sky. Breathe deeply as you energize and renew your body and spirit.*

# Soaring Like the Wind

*Thunderbird Woman*
*Recorded on* The Dawning—Chants of the Medicine Wheel

Soar- ing like the wind soar- ing like the wind on
wings of love you will my child soar thru the world.
Ah ha hi ya Ah ha hi ya Hi ah ah
Ha.

# All the Air is Sacred

*Recorded by Prana on* Second Chants © 1983

All the air is sa- cred, ev- 'ry breath we take, all the air is sa- cred,

ev- 'ry breath we take, u - - ni - - te the peo- ple, we are one

u - - ni - - te the peo- ple, we are one.

**Verse:**
All of life is sacred, every breath we take.
All the earth is sacred, every step we take.

## Purification With The Four Elements

### Earth Purification:

*Sit or squat on the earth in the center of a stone circle. Release all your unwanted energy out through the base of your spine and your feet. Let it be re-absorbed by the earth. Then, allow the earth's magnetic power to flow back into you through your feet and coccyx, bringing you into alignment and balance with the earth.*

*Dig a hole in the earth. Cover yourself with clay or mud to release toxins.*

**Give thanks for the purifying power of Earth.**

### Water Purification:

*Put salt into a bowl of water. Salt is a natural element that absorbs negativity. Sprinkle the water around you and others as well as your sacred space.*

*Stand under the rain, or a waterfall. Feel the healing waters cascading through you, cleansing your body and soul.*

**Give thanks for the purifying power of Water.**

### Fire Purification:

*Burn incense or an herbal mixture of sage, cedar, and sweetgrass (called 'Smudge') in a ceramic bowl or shell. Fan the smoke (with a feather or your hand) around you and others as you say prayers and call for protection. Direct the smoke to any area of your body you feel needs healing, as you visualize golden light flowing there.*

*Do the 'breath of fire, a rapid panting breath, repeating the sound 'Hu' over and over in a whisper or out loud. Feel the pumping action of the diaphragm and solar plexus as the fire breath purifies and oxygenates your whole system.*

**Give thanks for the purifying power of Fire.**

### Air Purification:

*Watch your breath. Let your exhale become longer. Release your thoughts; feel your mind become still. Allow new breath to enter spontaneously, as if the breath is breathing you, filling you with new life and vitality.*

*Add sound to your breath; open your voice. Direct your sounds to different parts of your body that need healing.*

*Send your prayers to the four directions on each breath.*

**Give thanks for the purifying power of Air.**

## The Four Elements Together

The following chants and dances work with the four elements together. Use them in your healing ceremonies and to create sacred space.

# The Earth, The Water, The Fire, The Air

A purification chant to use at the beginning or end of a ceremony. To call in the elements, change the words 'return, return' to 'come in, come in'. It is often sung with the Chumash wolf chant to balance male and female energy. (See Animal Kingdom chants in Chapter Three.)

**Dance:**
Stand or sit.
**The earth, the water, the fire, the air**
Hands at waist level, palms up. Move them up slowly toward the sky for four beats.
**Return, return, return, return**
Turn palms down. Move hands toward earth for four beats.
Continue moving hands in this pattern for the rest of the chant.
**Hey ye ye ye ye ye ye**–Raise energy up–male.
**Wo wo wo wo wo wo wo**–Ground energy down–female.

# Air I Am

*Andreas Corbin © 1982*
*Recorded on* All beings of the Earth*—EarthSpirit Community.*

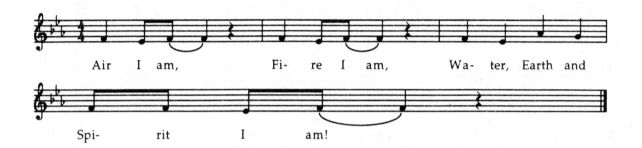

Air I am, Fi- re I am, Wa- ter, Earth and

Spi- rit I am!

**Verses:** Add your own
Breeze I am
Sun I am.
Brook, Mountain and
Goddess I am.

Maiden, I am
Mother, I am
Sister, lover, crone I am.

# Tall Trees, Warm Fire

*Tony Wrench*
*Recorded by Prana on* First Chants *© 1982*

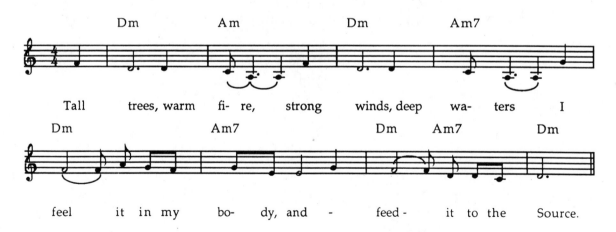

Tall trees, warm fi- re, strong winds, deep wa- ters I

feel it in my bo- dy, and - feed- it to the Source.

# Air Moves Us

*Cathleen Sheil, Moonsea, Prune*
*Recorded on* Chants–Ritual Music, *Reclaiming Community*

**Dance:**
**Air**—Wave hands freely above head
**Fire**—Clap hands percussively
**Water**—Make wave-like motion with hands to the left.
**Earth**—Place hands palms down or touch the earth drawing in
earth's magnetism.
**And the balance of the wheel goes round**—In a circle, put your
arms on the shoulders of those on either side and rock back and
forth.

# Earth and Ocean

*Mary Ann Fusco*
*Recorded on* Aradia's Songs for All Seasons © 1984

# Deep Deep You Are

*David Casselman* © 1981

# Spirit of the Wind

*Craig/ Star Williams*
*Recorded on* Uplifting the World, *Acoustic Medicine*

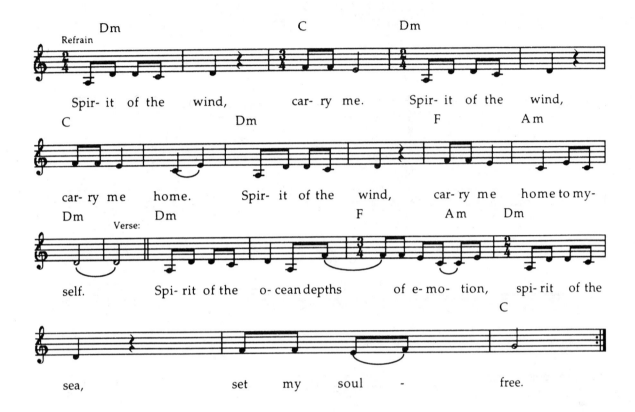

Spir- it of the wind, car- ry me. Spir- it of the wind,

car- ry me home. Spir- it of the wind, car- ry me home to my-

self. Spi- rit of the o- cean depths of e- mo- tion, spi- rit of the

sea, set my soul - free.

Sing the refrain alone if you wish, adding your own words such as 'Spirit of the Earth (sea, fire, wolf, etc) carry Me.'

**Verses:**

2. Spirit of the storm
help me be reborn.
Spirit of the rain,
wash away my pain.

4. Spirit of the Earth
help me with my birth.
Spirit of the land,
 hold me in your hand

3. Spirit of the sun
warm light healing me.
Spirit of the sky,
spread my wings and fly

5. Spirit of the river,
blessed forgiver.
Spirit of the shore,
shows me more and more

# Makowele

*Recorded on* Native American Ceremonial Chants

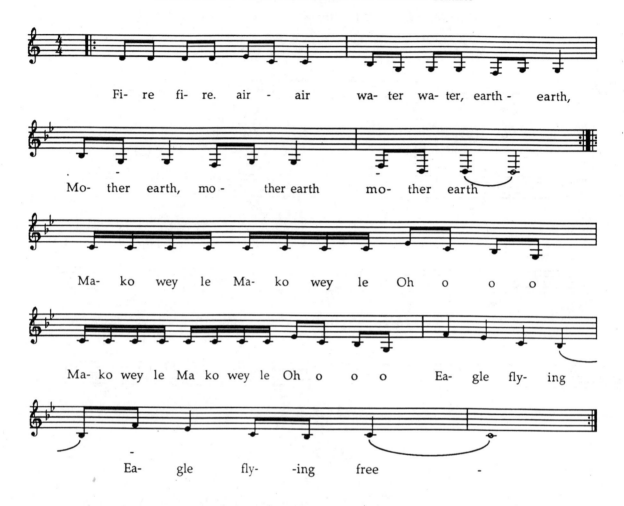

Fi- re fi- re. air - air wa- ter wa-ter, earth- earth,

Mo- ther earth, mo - ther earth mo - ther earth

Ma- ko wey le Ma- ko wey le Oh o o o

Ma- ko wey le Ma ko wey le Oh o o o Ea- gle fly- ing

Ea- gle fly- -ing free -

This chant calls in the elemental spirits and is often used in a sweat lodge. Sing it four or eight times. It is pronounced Mack—O—Well—Lay.

# Fire and Air

*Recorded by Libana on* A Circle is Cast © 1986

Dm Drone

Fi- re and air - Fi- re and air - Earth, wa- ter Earth, wa- ter

# We Come From de Water

We come    from    de wa- ter,    li-v ing    in    de    wa- ter,

go back    to    de wa-ter,    turn  de world - a- round.

We    come    from    de    wa-  ter,    go back    to    de wa- ter,

turn    de    world    a-    round.

A chant from Africa, popularized by Harry Belafonte. Add verses for each of the elements: 'We come from the earth, fire and sky (sky-eye), etc.' Add other lines as well such as River make the water, Water wash the river, Fire makes the sunlight, (turn de world around), Heart is of the river, Body is the mountain, Spirit is the sunlight. etc.

# Earth My Body, Water My Blood

*Recorded by Prana on* Return of the Mayflower © 1987/ 88

Round

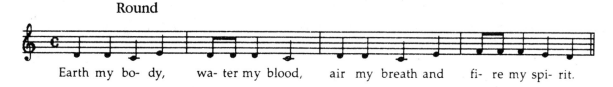

Earth my bo- dy,    wa- ter my blood,    air  my breath and    fi- re my spi- rit.

**Dance:**
**Earth my body**—Hands face the earth, or touch your body
**Water my blood**—Hands make wavelike motions out from heart.
**Air my breath**—Hands open out from mouth, reaching into space
**Fire my spirit**—Clap hands in front of third eye, sending fire upward.

# I Am Becoming You

*Michael Tierra*

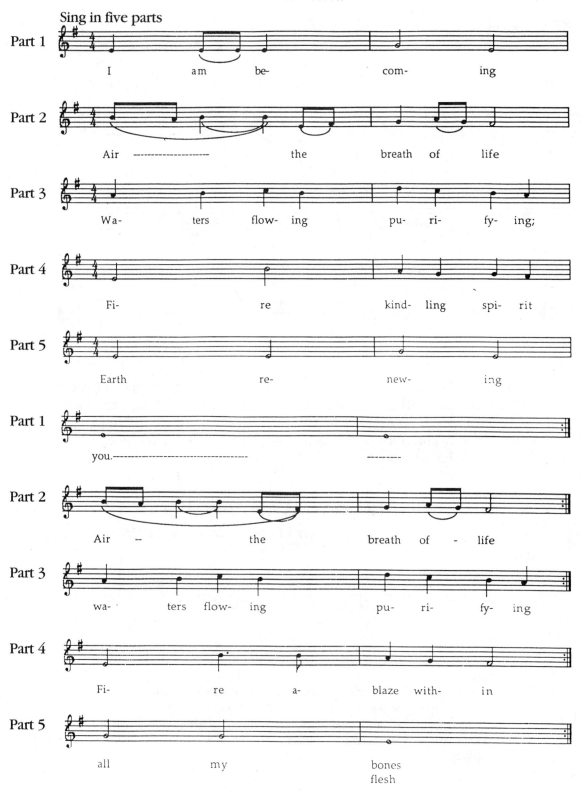

This a beautiful five part healing chant. Each line invokes one of the elements. You can substitute 'I am healing you' for 'I am becoming you'.

# Chapter Three

# Honoring All Our Relations

# Honoring All Our Relations

### Meditation—All Our Relations

*Sit quietly in a beautiful healing place in nature. Become aware of the life forms which surround you. Feel your oneness with them. Open all your senses; listen to the sounds, look at the colors, smell the fragrances, taste the flavors, and touch the textures.*

*Experience your deep connection with all the kingdoms. Ask for a message from the minerals, plants, animals and humans. Receive the guidance and wisdom of the ancient ones. Chant a simple prayer to honor and bless 'all your relations.'*

## Connecting with Nature

Native people believe that all living things have a soul and embody magical power which can guide us and keep us in balance. The chants in this section help us deepen our connection with nature, and all life.

# Rainbow Circle

*Chris Garland and Avril Harwood*
*Recorded by Prana on* Seven Seasons Suns, ©1984

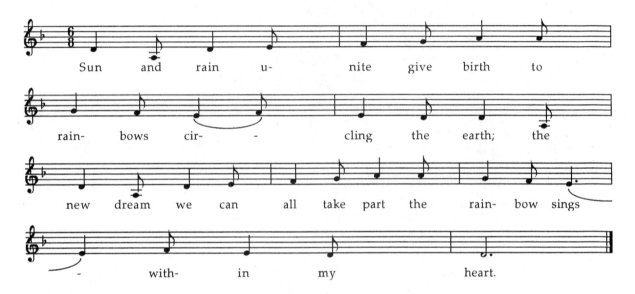

Sun and rain u- nite give birth to rain- bows cir - cling the earth; the new dream we can all take part the rain- bow sings - with- in my heart.

# Look at the Beauty

*Thunderbird Woman*
*Recorded on* The Dawning—Chants of the Medicine Wheel

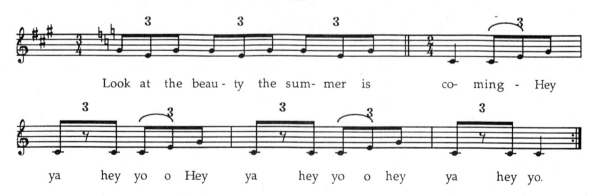

Look at the beau- ty the sum- mer is co- ming - Hey ya hey yo o Hey ya hey yo o hey ya hey yo.

Add words to this chant for each of the seasons. For example, 'the winter, spring, fall is coming.'

# Evening Breeze

*Recorded on* Coming Light —
Chants to Honor the Earth Mother © 1987

Eve- ning breeze, spi- rit song, sings to me when the

day is done. Mo- ther earth a- wak- ens me with the

heart beat of the sea.

# Morning Turns to Glory

Mor- ning turns to glo- ry, on the glow- ing should- ders of the

mount- ain. All the earth - is - still; all the

earth - is - still.

65

# Spirits Flying in the Sky

*Suryadas*

Spir- its fly - ing in the sky, thun- der in the ground. Wis- dom of the u- ni verse, old ones teach- ing me. Na- ture spi- rits sing-ing in my heart, op - en ing, call- ing me to you, on- ly you, on- ly you, on- ly you, on- ly you.

## Between Earth and Sky

The following chants help us come into harmony with Mother Earth and Father Sky and balance our masculine and feminine polarities. (See also Inner Peace and Harmony in Chapter Seven.)

### Meditation—Between Earth and Sky

*Imagine you have roots growing from the bottoms of your feet. Feel your roots extend deep into the earth, through the soil, the stones, the bedrock and subterranean waters into the fire at the core of the earth. As you breathe in, draw this inner earthfire up through your roots and circulate it through your whole body, into your legs, your pelvis, your belly, your chest, your head, arms, hands, and fingers. As you breathe out, release any tensions through your roots into the earth.*

*As you look up, become aware of a brilliant, glowing sun above you, symbolizing the Source of your being, your spiritual essence. Absorb the sun's warmth and light through the top of your head; feel it flowing through every cell of your body, affirming who you are. Experience your connection between Father Sky and Mother Earth as your energy rises from deep below you into the heavens and then circles back down again into the earth, through your roots.*

# Earth Child, Star Child

*By Clio from the Prana Collective*

Earth child - , Star child - , now is the time to o-pen our hearts,

with our feet - firm- ly on Grand- mo - ther earth with our feet -
with our arms - reach- ing for Grand- fa - ther Sky with our arms

firm- ly on Grand - mo - ther Earth.
reach- ing for Grand fa - ther Sky

Verse 1—Sing first line twice, then second line once.
Verse 2—Sing first line twice again, second line once, and so on.

# Sing a Song of the Earth/Sky

*Traditional*
*Recorded on* The Dawning—Chants of the Medicine Wheel

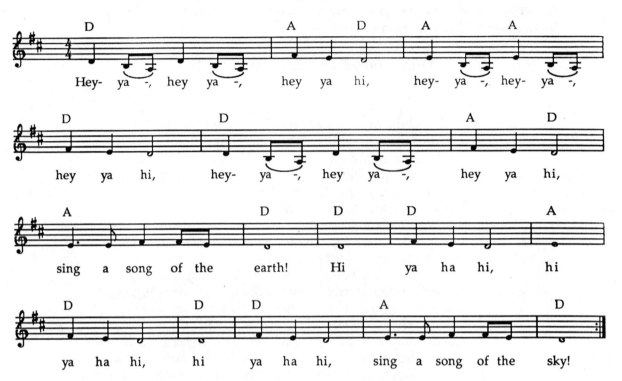

After everyone has sung it through twice, the women sing the verse to the earth while the men simultaneously sing the verse to the sky.

## Hopi Prayer

*I ask that this day*
*The Sky Father and the Earth Mother*
*Meet in my heart*
*That they will be inseparable*
*Today and forever more.*

Speak this daily at sunrise and sunset,
facing the sun, with arms uplifted.

# Mother I Feel You Under My Feet

*By Windsong*

Mo- ther I feel you un- der my feet, Mo- ther I hear your
heart beat He- ya he- ya he- ya he- ya he- ya he- yo,
he- ya he- ya he- ya he- ya he yo - -

**Dance:**

Throughout the dance(except the chorus), step rhythmically around the circle facing clockwise (all in same direction). Be aware of your feet on the earth.

**1. Mother, I feel you under my feet**—Hands/palms facing down toward the earth, connecting with the earth's energy.

**2. Mother, I hear your heart beat**—Hands come up and cross at the heart, beating up and down on chest in rhythm.

**Chorus**

**3. Heya Heya Heya Heya `Heya He Yo**—4 steps into center hands at sides,palms down connecting with earth energy (as in #1)

**4. Heya Heya Heya Heya `He Yo**—4 steps back, ( hands stay in same position )

**Verse: ( for male energy)**

**5. Father, I see you where the eagle flies**—Hands up high, palms and face turned towards the sky, connecting with the father energy.

**6. Spirit's gonna take me higher and higher**—Spin individually in place several times, with hands and head held high.

**Repeat chorus**

After everyone knows the full chant and dance, focus just on the mother lines #1 and #2, repeating them over and over. Then focus in the same way on the father lines #5 and #6. Try having just the women sing #1 and #2 ; then the men sing #5 and #6. Line # 6 is also effective repeated over and over by itself as you spin and spin raising the energy higher and higher. (Try doing verses alone without the chorus for a time) Finish the dance by unifying all the energies—singing the chant all the way through. At the end, ground the energy, with everyone kneeling down and touching the earth.

# Two Hands Hold The Earth

*Sarah Pirtle*
*Recorded on* Two Hands Hold the Earth © 1989

**Dance:** (By Sarah Pirtle)

1. Reach up one arm at a time on 'sky; sky sky'; 2. Stamp your feet on 'ground,ground ground.' 3. "What about my blood? It's from the sea'–sway arms and torso like waves; 4. 'And what about my bones? Like the mountains be.'–Make fists and strong movements. 5. 'And my hands,oh my hands, I believe with my hands I could hold this land'–(Clap to the beat) 6. 'My two hands hold the earth' (2x)–Cup your hands as if holding the earth and rotate the earth in a circle.

## Entering the Kingdoms

The following chants and meditations connect us with all the kingdoms. Try doing the meditations for each of the kingdoms like a shamanic journey. Have a friend beat steadily on a drum, or play a drumming tape. (See bibliography for reference.)

## Mineral Kingdom

The stones are the record holders for the Earth Mother. They hold within them all of the planet's memories and history. The next chants and meditations deepen our connection to the mineral kingdom, the stone people.

### Stone Power Meditation

*Go to or imagine a place where there are many stones and rocks, such as a river bank, beach or mountain trail. As you explore this landscape, look for a special rock or stone that attracts your attention, that seems to be calling out to be with you.*

*Sit down with this stone friend. Begin to examine it, look at its shape, size, and texture. Notice any markings on it. There may be lines and patterns that remind you of ancient faces or a long forgotten language. What history and memories does this stone hold? Close your eyes and attune to its essence, to its old wise spirit. Let the stone speak to you. Hear its story. Open to its guidance and teachings for you. Take time to be with it, for as long as you wish.*

*When you feel complete, thank the stone and say goodbye, leaving it an offering and acknowledging it as a special friend, helper and ally.*

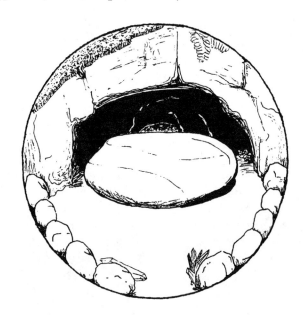

# The Rocks, the Stones and the Crystals

*Andrea and Tony Wrench*
*Recorded by Prana on* Rocks, Stones & Crystals © 1985

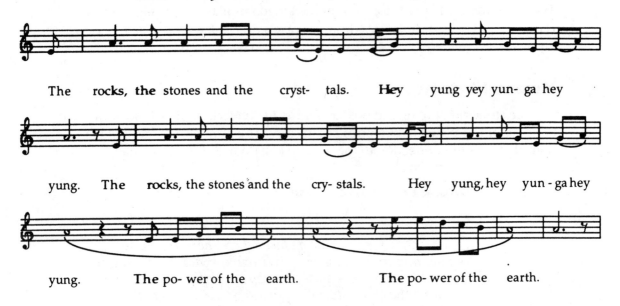

The rocks, the stones and the cryst- tals. Hey yung yey yun- ga hey

yung. The rocks, the stones and the cry- stals. Hey yung, hey yun - ga hey

yung. The po- wer of the earth. The po- wer of the earth.

# Life is Like a Crystal in the Sun

*© Lia Argo*
*Recorded on* Heartsongs

Life is like a crys- tal in the sun, we're all just co- lors of the

rain- bow, in the great white light we're one.

The crystal is the most powerful teacher of the mineral kingdom.

### Crystal Meditation

*Sit with a crystal in the sunlight. Look deep into it. Hold the crystal in your left hand and attune to its vibrations. Feel its power to expand your consciousness and clarify your thoughts. Think of a part of your life that needs more clarity, or something you would like to bring into manifestation. Hold this purpose or vision strongly as you meditate and chant with the crystal.*

## The Plant Kingdom

The plants are the givers of the earth. They provide for our basic food and sustenance and bring us powerful healing medicines. Native peoples understand how to maintain the ecological balance of nature, using only what they need. They communicate with the nature spirits, gathering plants in a sacred way and offering gifts back to Mother Earth in gratitude.

## Plant Spirit Meditation

*Go to or visualize a beautiful landscape full of lush vegetation, flowers, plants and trees.*

*Allow yourself to be drawn to one of these plants. Hear it calling out to you. Sit down next to it. Spend time looking at it; absorb its color, shape, leaves, flowers, stem, and trunk.*

*Then, close your eyes. Get in touch with its more subtle essence. Let the plant speak to you. Hear its story. Receive its guidance and teachings. Does it have a special gift or message for you? Interact with it as long as you wish. When you feel complete, thank it and say goodbye, leaving it an offering and acknowledging it as a special friend, helper and ally.*

# The Spirit of the Plant

*Lisa Thiel*

*Recorded on* Songs of the Spirit, © 1984

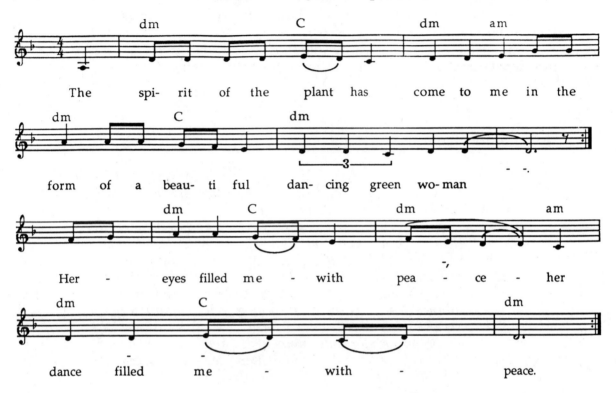

The spi- rit of the plant has come to me in the

form of a beau- ti ful dan- cing green wo- man

Her - eyes filled me - with pea - ce - her

dance filled me - with - peace.

# I Am the Spirit of the Tree

*Shekhinah Mountainwater*

As you sing this simple chant, walk over to a tree and hug it. Put your arms around its trunk, feeling its energy. Imagine yourself becoming one with the tree.

I am the spir - it of the tree -

**Verses:**

Add any other words you wish such as:
'I am the spirit of the sea, the earth', etc.

# My Roots Go Down

*Sarah Pirtle*
*Recorded on* Two Hands Hold the Earth © 1989

Plants, especially trees, are powerful symbols. They help us to feel our roots, connect with the earth and come into balance with all life. As you chant, breathe into your feet, imagine roots growing from them deep into the earth.

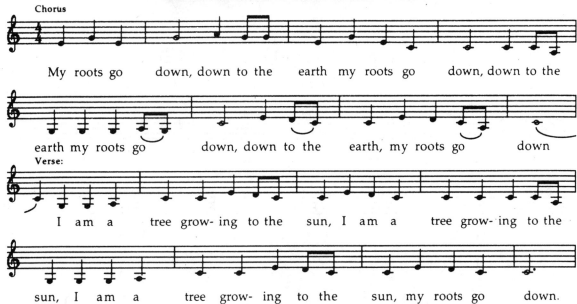

**Chorus**

My roots go down, down to the earth my roots go down, down to the earth my roots go down, down to the earth, my roots go down

**Verse:**

I am a tree grow-ing to the sun, I am a tree grow-ing to the sun, I am a tree grow-ing to the sun, my roots go down.

Substitute whatever words you wish, such as : ' I am a rock learning to be still, ' ' I am a tree living on the earth'

# She Will Bring The Buds in Spring

Oh she will bring the buds in the spring and laugh a- mong the flow- ers. In

sum- mer's heat her kis- ses are sweet she sings in leaf- y bow- ers. She

cuts the cane and ga- thers the grain when fruits of fall sur- round her. Her

bones grow old in the win- try cold, she wraps her cloak a- round her.

# Hinamay—Acorn Grinding Chant

*Native American*

Hi- na may - Hi- na may - Hi- na may chee wee yo Hi- na, Hi- na

hey- o, hi- na, hi- na hi- yo hi- yo.

# In the Garden

*Lia Argo* ©
*Recorded on* Heartsongs

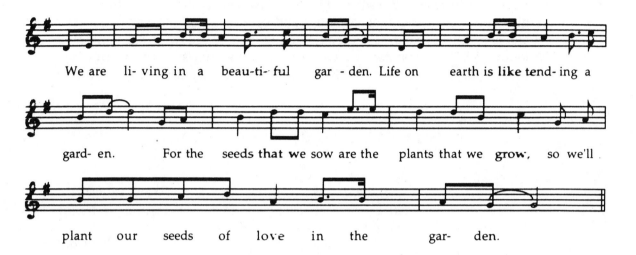

We are li- ving in a beau-ti- ful gar - den. Life on earth is like tend- ing a

gard- en. For the seeds that we sow are the plants that we grow, so we'll

plant our seeds of love in the gar- den.

**Verse:**

We will plant seeds of love in the garden
We will plant seeds of love in the garden
For the seeds that we grow
Are the plants that will grow
So we'll plant seeds of love in the garden.

We need sunshine and rain in the garden
We need earth, we need air in the garden
We need lots of loving care
To help the crops bear
And we'll harvest lots of love in the garden.

# Shewin Shewiliga

*NativeAmerican—Senecca Tradition*
*Recorded by Prana on* Return of the Mayflower,© 1987/88

This harvest song thanks the birds for bringing the healing herbs.

She win she wi li ga wa ha, she wi li ga wa ha, she wi lo wa.

She win she wi li ga wa ha, she wi li ga wa ha, she wi lo wa.

## The Animal Kingdom

Animals, like the rocks and plants, have spiritual power and are important healers and teachers for us. Native peoples recognize the special gifts and lessons each animal brings and believe we all have animal totems and allies closely guiding and empowering us. The following shamanic style journey will help you connect with an animal totem. Use a steady drum beat to take you on your journey. ( For more on shamanic journeys, see bibliography. )

### Power Animal Meditation

*In your imagination, find a passageway into the earth, such as a cave, hole in the ground or hollow tree. As you descend to this lower world, become aware of a landscape, opening up before you. Allow an image (or symbol) of an animal, reptile or bird to enter the landscape. Spend time being with this animal; tune into its deeper spirit. What does it have to teach you? How can it empower you at this time? Ask the animal for any message it may have for you; interact with it as long as you wish. When you feel complete, thank it and say goodbye, leaving it an offering. Acknowledge it as a special friend, helper and ally.*

# Fur and Feathers

This chant honors all creatures as God.

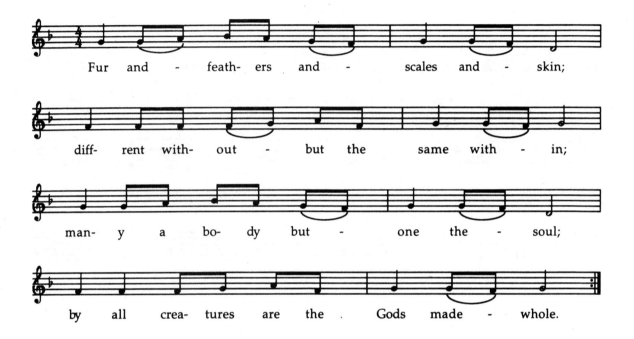

Fur and - feath-ers and - scales and - skin;

diff- rent with- out - but the same with - in;

man- y a bo- dy but - one the - soul;

by all crea- tures are the . Gods made - whole.

# Ka Yo—Song of the Bear

*Native American—Blackfoot Indian*

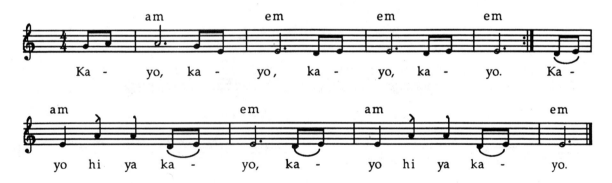

Ka - yo, ka - yo, ka - yo, ka - yo. Ka-

yo hi ya ka - yo, ka - yo hi ya ka - yo.

The bear is considered a sacred animal for many native people. It is a symbol of great strength and courage. Because it hibernates in caves in the winter, it is associated with feminine power, with introspection, and the ability to dream. It is also close to humans because it often stands on two legs. Ka—Yo (pronounced Fly—O) means 'bear' in Blackfoot.

# Najoli Win—Grandfather Bear

*Native American—Chumash Tradition*
*David Erdy*

Oh grand-fath-er bear, Oh won't you come here. Oh

Grand-fath-er bear, Oh, won't you come here, eh ya eh ya

eh ya.

**Verse:**
Najoli Win
Najoli Na 2x
Eh ya eh ya eh ya. Eh
Can substitute: O Grandmother bear, won't you lie here, etc.

# Ya Na Ho

Ya- na ho- way- ah, ho ay - nay. Ya- na ho- way ah, ho ay - nay.

Ho- way- ah, ho ay - nay    Hey - nay    Ya- na ho- way ah, ho ay - nay.

**Verse:**
Oh, Lord make me like a strong bear.
Oh, Lord make me like a strong bear.
This I pray, Lord. Make me strong
Oh, make me like a strong bear.

## Heya Heya Weya
*Native American Wolf Chant*

Hey- a, wey- a, hey- a, hey- a, wey- a, hey- a,

hey- ya ya, he he ya    hey ya ya he he yah,    ah

Wolves are the teachers, and pathfinders. They are very loyal, have a strong sense of family and tribe, and mate for life. It is the Wolf Spirit that sings the moon into to sky.

## Hey Ye Ye
*Native American Wolf Chant*

W o  hey  ye   ye   ye   ye   ye ye   ye    wo  wowo  wo   wo   wo  wo
Wo   wo   wo   wo   wo   wo   wowo   wo     ye   ye ye   ye    ye   ye  ye

The words ' Wo wo wo wo wo wo wo' and 'Ye ye ye ye ye ye ye' honor the he and she wolves respectively, the male and female aspects of our being. Alternate the two lines. It can also be sung with the chant 'The Earth the Fire the Water the Air 'and combined with simple hand movements. See Chapter Two for details.

## Buffalo

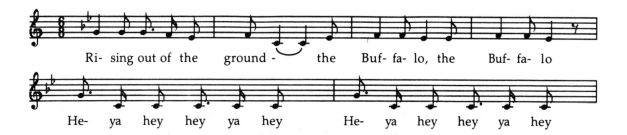

Ri- sing out of the    ground -   the   Buf- fa- lo, the   Buf- fa- lo

He- ya  hey  hey  ya  hey    He- ya  hey  hey  ya  hey

# Eewa Beleyo— Pygmy Elephant Song

*Adapted by Michael Tierra*

Ee wa be le yo    ee oo wa be le.    Ee wa    le be le yo.    Ee wa    le be le

# White Dolphin Swimming

© *Susan Elizabeth Hale*
*Recorded on* Circle the Earth with Song

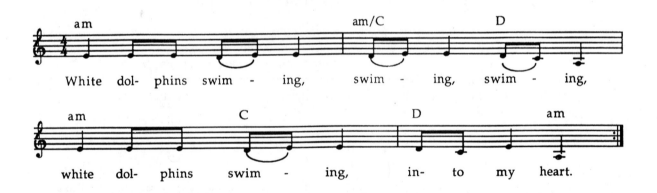

This simple chant calls to the dolphins who teach us about the power of breath and sound, how to open our hearts, contact our inner child and communicate telepathically. The chant can also be used to invoke the spirit of many different animals and bring them into your heart.

**Verse:**
Add your own words such as 'brown bear dancing', 'dappled fawn skipping', 'grey rabbit hopping', 'black snake slithering', etc.

# Epona—Song to the White Horse Goddess

*By Ivo Dominguez Jr.*

Waves crash,    hoof beats on the sand,   E- pon · a

This chant invokes the Celtic white horse goddess. The spirit of the horse represents our power and freedom.

**Verses:**
Winds Gust
Manes ablaze go free—E-pona

White mares
Spirit of the wild—E-pona

# Little Deer Song

*Native American–Piute tradition*
*Recorded on* Native American Ceremonial Chants

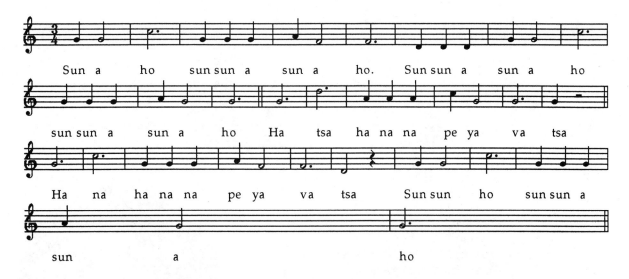

Sun a   ho   sun sun a  sun a  ho.  Sun sun a  sun a  ho

sun sun a  sun a  ho  Ha tsa  ha na na  pe ya  va tsa

Ha na  ha na na  pe ya  va tsa  Sun sun  ho  sun sun a

sun   a     ho

The deer teaches the healing power of gentleness and unconditional love.

# Wendeya Ho

Honors the Butterfly and the power of the Air.

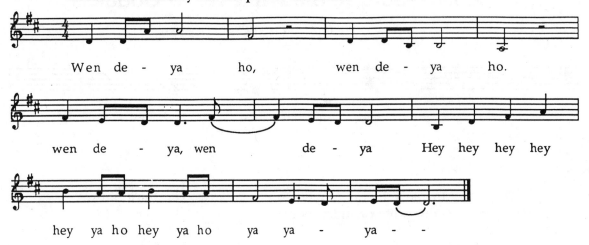

Wen de - ya ho, wen de - ya ho.

wen de - ya, wen de - ya Hey hey hey hey

hey ya ho hey ya ho ya ya - ya - -

# Be a Butterfly

*David Casselman © 1982–83*

Here's a song you can all join in. Be a but- ter fly there's no tom -

mo- row Fly- ing thru the air in the sun- shine can you

see what I - mean.

**Verses:**
Substitute for the first line:
2. The air so clear and the sun so bright.
3. Yesterday was just a puff of the wind.
4. The answer lies in who you are.
5. Always here and always now.
6. Life is easy if you just let go.
7. Be a dancer of the universe.

# Condor Song
*Ophidia*

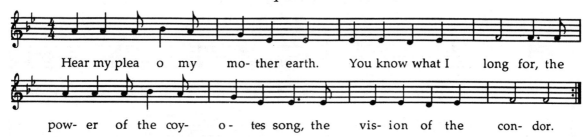

Hear my plea o my mo- ther earth. You know what I long for, the

pow- er of the coy- o- tes song, the vis- ion of the con- dor.

**Verses:**
The wisdom of the rattlesnake
The kind heart of the dove
Let me walk in a mindful way
On your path of beauty and love

# Spinning Around The Wheel
*Thunderbird Woman—Bear Tribe*
*Recorded on* The Dawning

As you create a medicine wheel, call in different animal totems and the
gifts they bring. Make up your own verses.

Spin- ning a- ro- und, spin- ning a ro- und, spin- ing ar- ound the wheel.

**Verses:**
**Chorus**— Sing chorus through twice between verses. Use the
words noted above for the first time through; second time through
substitute "turning" for "spinning".
**Call** —I am the snowgoose, I am the snowgoose
flying around the wheel
**Response**—You are the snowgoose, you are the snowgoose
flying around the wheel
Repeat as a call and reponse, adding the following verses after each
chorus:
Cougar—stalking around the wheel; Otter—swimming;
Brown Bear— walking, Snake— slithering; Elk— daning;
Deer— running, bee— buzzing etc.

# Be Like A Bird

*Recorded on* The Fire Within *By Libana*

Be like a bird who halt-ting in her flight on a limb too slight, feels it

give-way be-neath her, yet sings, sings, know-ing she has wings, yet

sings, sings, know-ing she has wings.

# Blue Heron Song

*Recorded on* Native American Ceremonial Chants

Wey o wa hey. Wey o wa hey. Wey o wa hey o wey wey o wey. Wey o

wa hey, I am cal-ling. Wey o wa hey o wey wey o wey.

**Verse 2**
Wey yo wa hey–Sing 2x
Wey yo wa hey o wey wey o wey
I am calling
Wey yo wa hey
Wey yo wa hey o wey wey o wey

# As the Swan Sings

**Traditional**

*Recorded on* Songs of the Heart, *Malcolm Stern and Stairway* 1988

As the swan sings la la la la   la la la la   la la la la

The Swan is associated with receptive feminine energy, intuition and grace. By invoking the swan you can learn to surrender to the rhythm of the universe, and open to expanded states of awareness.

**Verses:**
With this chant, add names of other birds you wish to invoke such as 'As the thrush, robin, wren, etc. sing.', or try 'As the Owl calls, Hoo, Hoo, Hoo.'

# Owl Song

Owl I sing to   your black tal-ons   Owl I sing to your   yel-low eyes.

Moon's eyes   owl's eyes   the   cold clear eyes up-   on my dreams.

The owl is associated with the mysteries of the night, with clairvoyance and wisdom. It is the night hunter. As you invoke the spirit of the owl, ask it to release your fear of the dark. Call for wisdom and clarity of vision.

# Weyniya
*Hopi Eagle Dance*

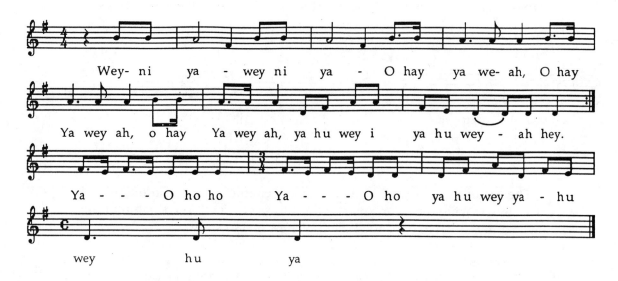

Wey- ni ya - wey ni ya - O hay ya we-ah, O hay

Ya wey ah, o hay Ya wey ah, ya hu wey i ya hu wey - ah hey.

Ya - - O ho ho Ya - - O ho ya hu wey ya - hu

wey hu ya

# I Circle Around
*Native American Eagle Chant—Arapahoe Ghost Dance Tradition*

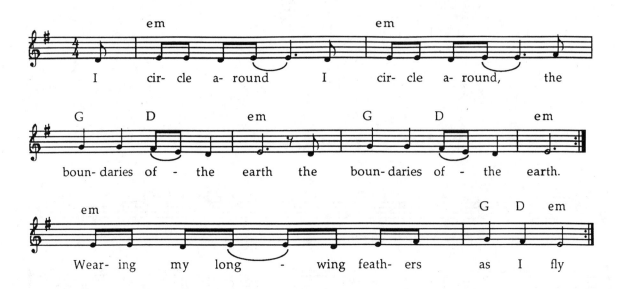

I cir- cle a- round I cir- cle a- round, the

boun- daries of - the earth the boun- daries of - the earth.

Wear- ing my long - wing feath- ers as I fly

The eagle teaches us of the spirit realm. Soaring above the mundane levels of life, it helps us develop the qualities of clarity, clear vision, detachment and discrimination. Eagle feathers are considered very sacred. It is said that one cannot lie in the presence of an eagle feather.

**Dance:**
**I Circle Around, etc.** Do the Ghost dance step version #1 (Step R, stamp L, Step L, stamp R) around circle, holding hands. Repeat 2x
**Wearing my long wing feathers, etc**. Continue Ghost dance step turning individually in a small circle. Spread arms out like eagle wings, as you rock side to side. Repeat 2x.

88

# We All Fly Like Eagles

*Native American—Arapahoe Ghost Dance*

Sing as a call and response, with group repeating each phrase a
second time. Try the Ghost Dance step as in *I Circle Around*.

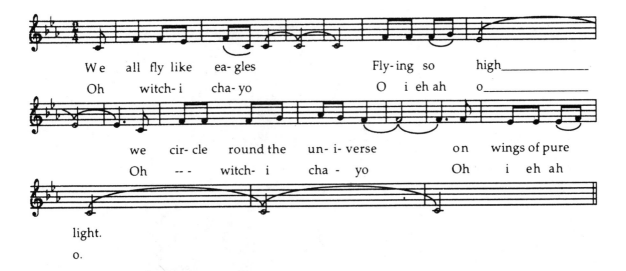

## Calling the Ancestors

The following chants call in the spirit and power of our ancestors and help us to open to ancient wisdom and guidance.

As preparation, do a simple ritual to communicate with an ancestor. Look at a picture of one of your ancestors. Light a candle for them, and chant their name. This is particularly powerful to do on October 31, the Celtic festival called Samhain (Hallowe'en or All Hallow's Eve). It is said that at this time the veil between the worlds is very thin. We are closer to the world of the dead, to beings on the other side.

### Meditation—Calling the Ancestors

*Sit in a sacred circle at night. Allow your consciousness to flow back to a time when your ancestors walked the earth. Let images of their faces emerge; what were their lives like? What do your ancestors have to teach you? What can you share with them? Ask to meet one of them. Take as long as you wish to speak and interact with this old wise one asking for his/her guidance, and wisdom*

*When you are ready, return slowly, bringing back the essence of your ancestral journey.*

# We Are an Old People

*By Morning Feather/Will Shepardson*
*Recorded on* Chants–Ritual Music

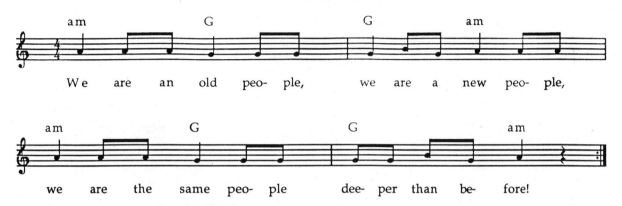

We are an old peo- ple, we are a new peo- ple,

we are the same peo- ple dee- per than be- fore!

**2nd verse:**

> Cauldron of changes
> Blossom of bone
> Ark of eternity
> Hole in the stone

Also sing with the chant *Isis, Astarte, Hecate, Demeter, Kali, Innana* (See Chapter Four) to invoke the power and wisdom of these ancient Goddesses. The melodies are similar. Add the verses for the male Gods if you wish. (See Chapter Five.) The following words can also be used as a counterpoint.

> I am a strong woman
> I am a story woman
> I am a healer
> My soul will never die.

> I am a gentle man
> I am a wild man (or green man)
> I am a warrior
> My soul will never die.

**Dance:**
Do a simple grandmother step, weaving circles in and out or creating a spiral. Look deep into others eyes, seeing all the ageless 'faces'. A power dance can also be done, with each person taking a turn in the center. (See Power Dance in Chapter 1.)

# Blood of the Ancients

*Words by Ellen Klaver Music Charlie Murphy*
*Recorded on* Canticles of Light

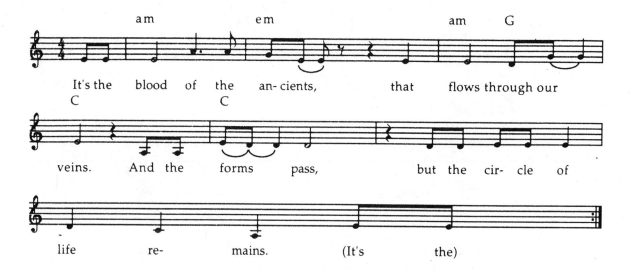

am          em          am     G

It's the blood of the an-cients, that flows through our

C          C

veins. And the forms pass, but the cir- cle of

life re- mains. (It's the)

**Dance:**

Divide group into equal numbers with partners.
All stand in a circle facing in. .

**1. It"s the blood of the ancients**
**2. that  flows through our veins.**

All move together in a circle. Let your hands be free, palms facing down, connecting with the energy of the earth. Do a side step. As you step to the side with your R foot, bend your knee and lean your whole body to the R into the movement. Let your head sway down and up to the R as well. Feel yourself deeply rooted and connected to the earth. Then let the L foot join the right. With each side-step feel your connection to the ancestors, to all the ancient wise ones who also walked the earth. .

**3. And the forms pass,**

The partner on left side of couple will be moving, the other partner stays still. The moving partner releases their hands and moves into the circle facing partner. The moving partner takes three small rhythmic side steps to left passing partner in circle Both partners have hands raised at shoulder level palms facing each other (not touching)and maintain eye contact. They look deeply into each others eyes, seeing the essence of the person beyond their form. .

**4. But the circle of life remains.**

The moving partner rejoins and closes the circle turning back around, again facing into the center of the circle joining hands with neighbors. The person on the right will become their new partner. Everyone side steps together holding hands in one circle feeling their oneness and connection with all, with the circle of life. Continue side stepping together repeating the last line once more affirming 'Yes, the circle of life remains'. Raise hands up to W. Then  begin cycle again.

You can do the dance more freely in a line, circle or snake pattern. Embody the spirit of the ancestors any way that you feel it, keeping with the grandmother step. Look into the faces of others passing by you. Make eye contact with each person as you encounter them, seeing beyond their present form into their ageless ancient dimension.

If you have a large enough group, divide into two circles, an inner circle of women (facing out) and an outer circle of men (facing in) preferably equal in number so the partners are facing each other. The circles move in opposite directions, bringing in the balance of male and female energy.

# Ehara

This is a Maori proverb from New Zealand. It means 'Love is handed down from our ancestors'.

# Come Forward and Meet Us

*Jim Berenholtz*
*Recorded on* Turquoise Waters © 1986

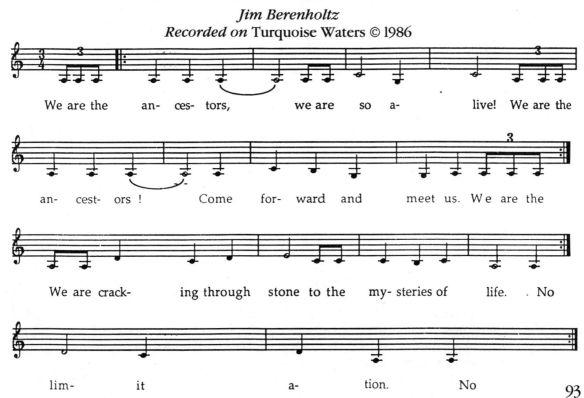

# To the Old Man / Woman of Creation

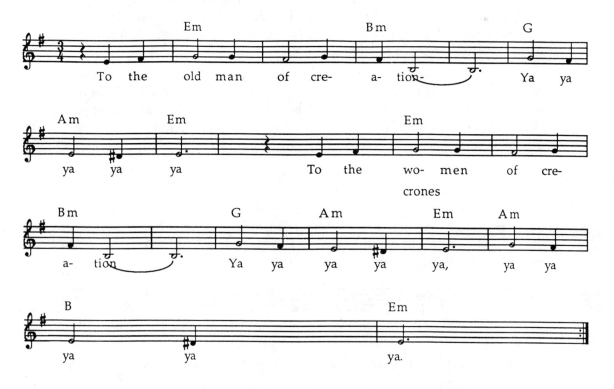

# We Ask the Ancient Women

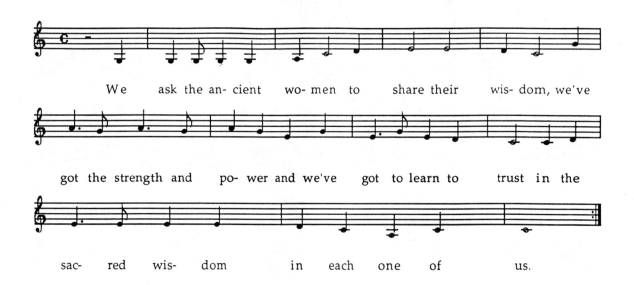

**Verses:**
Substitute:'the ancient men, or the ancient ones.' Use this chant to
honor the elders in a circle by chanting, 'We ask the aged (or elder)
women, men, etc. to share their wisdom'.

# Ancestors

*Tony Wrench*
*Recorded by Prana on* Rocks, Stones and Crystals, © 1985

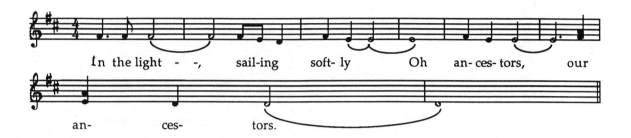

In the light - -, sail-ing soft-ly Oh an-ces-tors, our an-ces-tors.

**Verses:**
Coming home from Sirius, Oh Ancestors
Travelling from Seven Sisters, Oh Ancestors
With the light, speaking softly, Oh, Ancestors

# O Grandmother, I Feel You Lift Me Up

Instead of 'O Grandmother', substitute 'O grandfather', 'O great mystery' or 'O ancient ones.'

O grand-mo-ther, I feel you lift me up and car-ry me - home.

**Dance:**
As you chant, stand in the center of a sacred circle. Kneel down putting your head on the earth. Slowly stand up as you raise arms, hands and head upward toward the heavens on the word 'home'. This can be done as a solo dance or with a group holding hands as they rise up together.

# Wey O Wey, Grandmother

*Recorded on* Native American Ceremonial Chants

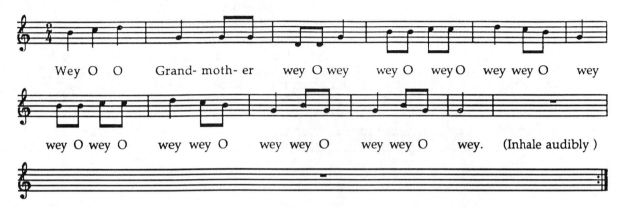

(Exhale deeply and audibly)

Add other verses with words such as 'Grandfather' 'Great Spirit' or lines for the elements like 'Air Spirit' After singing the chant through each time, take an audible breath, a deep inhale and exhale feeling profound devotion. Cover your heart with your hands as you inhale—drawing energy inside you through your heart; as you exhale, open hands out from your heart in front of you, sending energy out.

# O Grandmother, We are Calling to You

# Chapter Four

# Woman Power

# Woman Power

## Meditation—Woman Power

*Imagine yourself in a landscape which represents the feminine aspect of your being. Allow images and symbols to unfold in your landscape that are connected with your female power. What are the dominant elements, colors, sounds, shapes, and smells? As you look around, you may discover a deep pool of water, a cave, lush valleys and hills, or the full moon shining. Notice what animals, plants and stones are there. Take time to explore, bringing in rich detail, opening all your senses.*

*Become aware of other women there with you, women of all ages and colors. They are coming toward you now, greeting you, and forming a circle around you. As you look at these women, you see the faces of your female ancestors; of women you have known; of powerful, wise women; of young maidens, mothers and grandmothers; of heroines and Goddesses. Take some time to be with them and share in any way that you wish.*

*Then, focus on one woman who represents an ideal for you. Invite her to stand before you. Let your eyes meet. Interact with her. What does she have to teach you? Ask her what you need at this time for your growth and to come more fully into your woman power.*

*Look inside yourself for the energy or symbol that represents your inner woman. Begin to embody and express this female energy, allowing sound and movement to emerge. What messages and teachings do you receive?*

It is the balance of the masculine and feminine within each of us that brings us into wholeness. The feminine is associated with nurturance, receptivity, intuition, feelings and the unconscious. The masculine is associated with action, passion, directed will, intellect and conscious thought. Women's mysteries center around their bodies, their reproductive power and inner life while men's mysteries center more on their actions in the world, on their becoming heroes and warriors.

In the next two chapters, chants and meditations are presented to help explore our feminine and masculine energies and discover the qualities we need to bring ourselves into balance and inner harmony.

## Women and Wisdom

In the earliest civilizations, women were honored for their wisdom and their power to create and sustain the physical and spiritual web of life. Recent archeological findings show us that the first cultures of the world were matriarchal, led by women. These societies worshipped Nature and the earth and existed in peace and harmony for thousands of years. (See reference for Marija Gimbutas in bibliography.) Their supreme deity was seen as female, as Goddess, as Divine mother. With increasing urbanization and the rise of patriarchy a new world view took hold; the feminine spirit went underground. Women were persecuted and subjugated; most lost touch with their power and wisdom. It is only in recent years that women and men have begun to rediscover their ancient heritage and reclaim the feminine aspects of their being.

The following chants celebrate women's wisdom and power, and explore different feminine images and archetypes.

# Woman am I

*Traditional—adapted from Blessed Am I*

100

# Woman Am I # 2

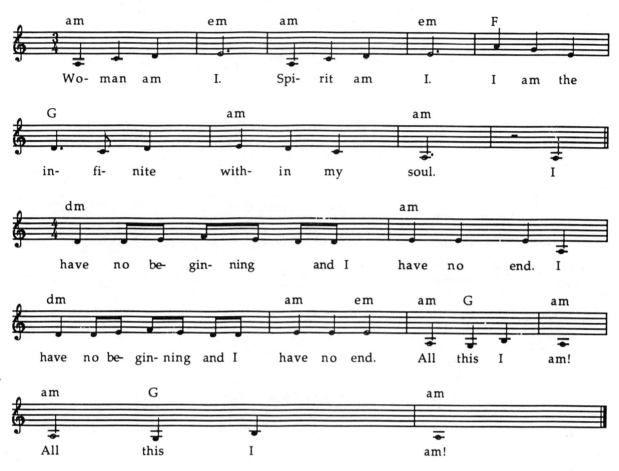

The original words of this song are 'Blessed am I, Spirit am I' Replace first line to create different affirmations, such as 'Beauty am I, Power am I.'

# Blessed is She

# Yana Wana Yana

*Native American Church*
*Recorded on* The Circle, In Search of Our Native Roots, 1980

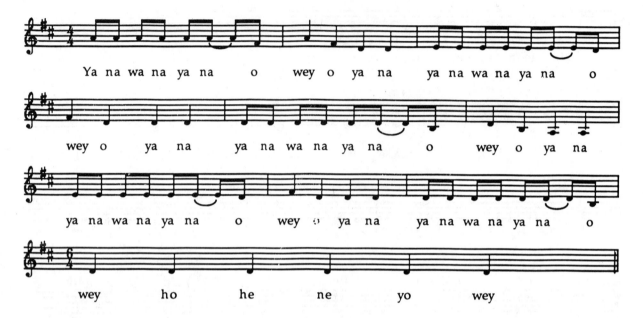

Ya na wa na ya na   o   wey o ya na   ya na wa na ya na   o

wey o   ya na   ya na wa na ya na   o   wey o ya na

ya na wa na ya na   o   wey o ya na   ya na wa na ya na   o

wey   ho   he   ne   yo   wey

**Verse:** (English)
Woman, wisdom, woman O wey O wisdom—sing four times
Woman, wisdom, woman O wey ho hey ne yo weh.

**Dance:**
**Yana wana yana o wey o yana** (4x) —Move around circle doing ghost dance step (version #1 0r #2) Hold hands in W position.
**O wey ho hey ne yo wey** — Do the same step but more strongly as a stamp.

The following *Witch Song* comes from the witchcraft movement, experiencing a revival today. It is important for us to reclaim the word *witch*; to associate it with true wisdom, positive power and healing. W*itch* originally comes from the Celtic word Wicca (pronounced wick-eh). It means the wise one, the one who practices the craft of the wise. Witches (predominantly women) worshipped nature and the Goddess. With the rise of Christianity, especially in Europe, witches came to be seen as heretics, as a threat to the power of the Church and the growing patriarchy. Many were persecuted and murdered. The height of the witch hunts occurred from the 14th to 18th centuries, killing between nine and eleven million people. It was not until 1951 that the last anti–witch law in England was repealed.

# The Witch Song

*Bonnie Lockhart,* ©1982

**Verses:**

When women had babies the witches were there
to hold them and help them and give them care.
Witches knew stories of how life began.
Don't you wish you could be one? Well, maybe you can.

Some people thought that the witches were bad.
Some people were scared of the power they had.
But power to help and to heal and to care
isn't something to fear, it's a pleasure to share.

# Snake Woman

*Starhawk* ©
*Recorded on* Chants–Ritual Music, *Reclaiming Community*

This catchy chant is done best as a call and response. Repeat each line twice. Make up your own verses.

Snake wo-man   shed-ding  her skin   shed-ding, shed-ding   shed-ing  her skin

**Verses:** (Repeat pattern)
Bird Woman taking flight.
Star Woman shining bright.
Moon Woman riding the night.
Blossom Woman opening wide.
**More verses by Snake Dancer:**
Rain Woman soaking the earth.
Tree Woman rooted in earth.
Tree Woman touching the core,
etc.

In pre-patriarchal Goddess religions, the snake was considered a sacred symbol for creative power and healing. Images of snakes and spirals are seen in many of the ancient temples throughout the world. The snake is a powerful symbol of life and renewal, regularly shedding its skin in much the same way as a women sheds her blood every month.

Hecate and Kali, goddesses associated with crone wisdom, with death and transformation, were often depicted with snakes in their hair. Ishtar was said to be covered by scales. The great Earth Mother goddess Demeter was attended in her temple at Eleusis by a snake called Kychreus. In the Hindu religions, the divine female presence within each of us, known as Kundalini, is depicted as a snake coiled at the base of the spine, waiting to be awakened.

The following snake meditation and dance can be part of a woman's empowerment ceremony, to help her get more in touch with her sexual/creative energy, her womb and snake power. Use live or taped shamanic drumming.

### Snake Power Meditation

*Imagine yourself in a powerful place in nature or in an underworld landscape.*

*Allow an image of a snake to emerge. Bring in as much detail as you can.*

*Begin to interact with the snake. Your encounter may be verbal or very physical. See what you have to learn from each other. What messages, or gift does the snake have for you?*

### Snake Power Dance

*In a stone circle, make an image of a coiled snake/serpent.*

*Stand on the snake image. Open to the snake power moving through you up from your feet.*

*Follow the steady pulse of a drumbeat. Let a dance and chant begin as you merge more and more with the spiralling energy of the snake.*

*Incorporate sounds, such as hissing, into your dance.*

Snake Goddess from
Knossos: 1600 B.C.

# White Buffalo Woman

Lisa Thiel

*Recorded on* Songs of the Spirit © 1984

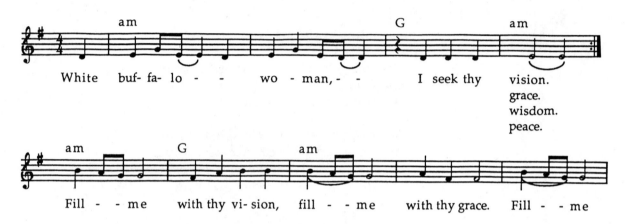

White buf- fa- lo - - wo - man, - - I seek thy vision.
grace.
wisdom.
peace.

Fill - - me with thy vi - sion, fill - - me with thy grace. Fill - - me

with thy wis- dom , fill - me - - with thy peace.

White Buffalo Woman is honored in the Lakota tradition as a woman of great wisdom and medicine power. The Lakota myth describes how Buffalo Woman brought the sacred medicine pipe to the people and taught them how to pray. The bowl of the pipe represents female power, the receptacle. The stem is the male energy. When bowl and stem are put together and tobacco (the most sacred plant to the Native Americans) is smoked, the balance of male and female, of earth and spirit is created. The Buffalo is considered one of the most sacred animals. It is a major source of sustenance—providing many gifts from its body.

The following chants and dances call in the spirit of Changing Woman, honored in many Native American traditions. She helps us move through our life transitions and brings protection and blessings. Changing Woman is associated with Spider Woman, considered among the people of the American South West as creatress of the world, weaver of life. It is said that Spider Woman created the world through the power of her thought, by breathing and singing it into existence.

# She Changes Everything She Touches
*Starhawk* ©

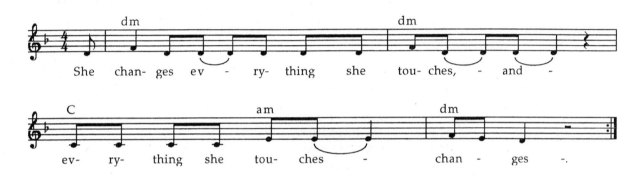

This chant is used by many groups on its own. It is the original chorus of *Kore's Chant* but has also inspired other songs and verses, such as *Changing Woman*.

# We are Changers
*Starhawk* ©

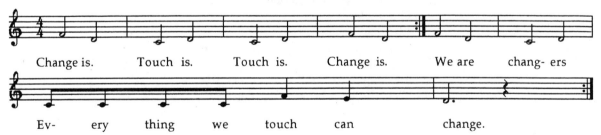

This is part of *She Changes Everything She Touches*. Sing it as a counterpoint or on its own.

**Verse:**
We are changers,
everything we touch is changing.
Change us. Touch us.
Touch us. Change us.

# Kore's Chant
*Starhawk* ©
*Recorded on* Chants–Ritual Music–*Reclaiming Community*

Sing these verses with the chorus of *She Changes Everything She Touches.*

Her    name can- not be -    spok- en.    Her face was not -    for- got- ten.

Her po- wer is    to    op- en.    Her    pro- mise    can ne- ver be    bro- ken.

**Verses:**

All seeds she deeply buries
She weaves the thread of seasons
Her secret darkness carries
She loves beyond all reason
**Chorus**
All sleeping seeds she wakens,
The rainbow is Her token
Now winter's power is taken
In love all chains are broken
**Chorus**
Everything lost is found again
in a new form, in a new way.
Everything hurt is healed again,
in a new time, in a new day.
(This verse works well sung alone as a healing chant—
see also Chapter Six.)
**Chorus**
Bright as a flower and strong as a tree
With our love and with our rage
Breaking our chains so we can be free
With our love and with our rage.

**Changing Woman Meditation**

*As you chant, meditate on change and what it means in your life. Think of your power to create your reality in each moment. Call on the spirit of Changing Woman to guide and bless you. Leave her an offering of cornmeal, symbol of prosperity, abundance and good fortune.*

# Changing Woman

*Adele Getty*

Sing these verses with the chorus of *She Changes Everything She Touches.*

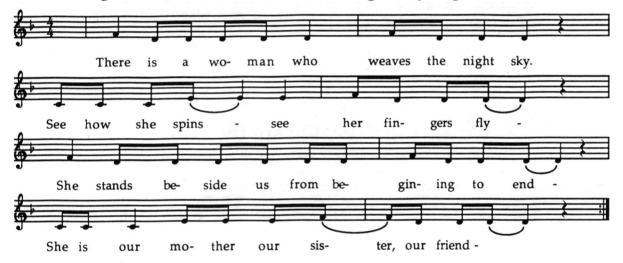

There is a wo-man who weaves the night sky.

See how she spins - see her fin-gers fly -

She stands be-side us from be-gin-ing to end -

She is our mo-ther our sis-ter, our friend -

**Verses:**

There was a time before we were born,
we were the calm in the eye of the storm.
We had a memory oh so deep,
about the truth and the beauty so sweet.

Man and woman passion ran wild,
they gave birth to a freedom child
We are the children of love and light.
We'll guide the children through the perilous night.
Lift up our hearts and raise our voices,
let the people know all of the choices.

She is the weaver, and we are the web.
She is the needle and we are the thread.
She weaves within us from begining to end,
Our great mother, our sister, our friend.

# Grandmother Spider Woman

*Ariana Lighteningstorm*
*Recorded on* Alchemy *by Kiva* © 1993

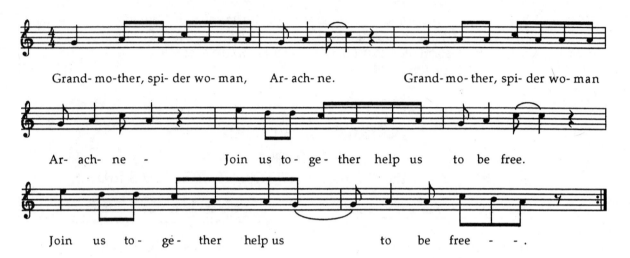

Grand- mo-ther, spi- der wo- man,    Ar- ach- ne.    Grand- mo-ther, spi- der wo- man

Ar- ach- ne -    Join us to- ge- ther help us    to be free.

Join    us to- gé- ther    help us    to    be    free  -  .

# We are the Flow, We are the Ebb

*Shekhinah Mountainwater*

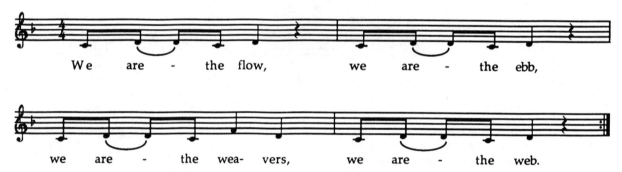

W e    are  -  the flow,    we    are  -  the ebb,

we    are  -  the wea- vers,    we    are  -  the web.

**Dance:**
Begin with a chain of dancers holding hands. The leader then
creates a spiral and moves between the others in a chain, weaving
in and out. As part of the dance or ritual, a ball of yarn can be used
to weave a web. It is passed from person to person, woven in front
of one, then behind the next, creating a web. Focus on what you
are weaving into your life Use red yarn to symbolize women's
power and vitality.
**Verses:**
We are the weavers, we are the web.
We are the spiders, we are the thread.

We are the spiders, we are the thread.
We are the witches back from the dead

# Spiralling into the Center

Sing this as a separate chant or as a counterpoint to *We are the Flow, We are the Ebb.* Do it with a spiral dance.

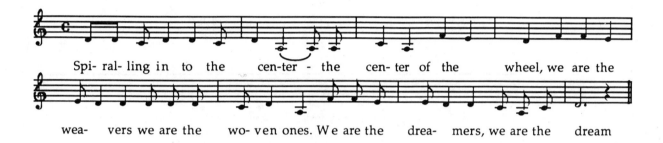

Spi- ral- ling in to the    cen-ter - the    cen- ter of the    wheel, we are the

wea-    vers we are the    wo- ven ones. We are the    drea-    mers, we are the    dream

# Lady Weave Your Circle Tight

Round

La- dy weave your    cir- cle tight    Fill us with your    ho-ly -    light

ea- rth, air -    fi- re and wa- ter    bind us to    you

This is done to the same melody as the chant *Love, Love, Love, Love.* (See Chapter Six.) Use it to create a sacred circle.

## Sisterhood

The following chants celebrate sisterhood and the unity of all women.

# Sure as the Wind

*Terry Dash ©*
*Recorded by Libana on* A Circle is Cast © 1986

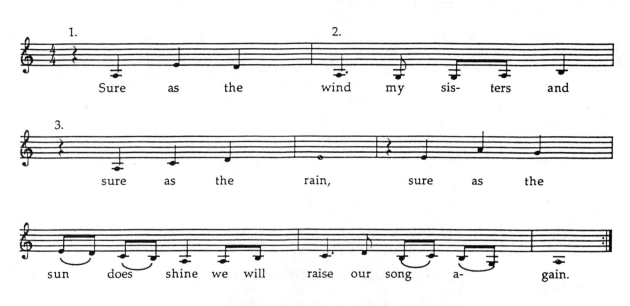

Sure as the wind my sis-ters and sure as the rain, sure as the sun does shine we will raise our song a-gain.

# We Are Sisters On A Journey

*Marlena Fontenay © 1981*

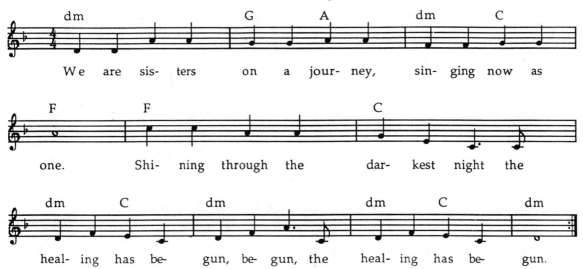

**Verses:**

We are sisters on a journey ,
singing in the sun,
remembering the ancient ones,
the women and the wisdom,
the women and the wisdom.

We are sisters on a journey
standing at the door.,
remebering what passed long ago
Let's turn the key once more.
Let's turn the key once more.

We are sisters on a journey
watching life unfold,
sharing warmth of heart and hands,
The knowledge of the old,
the knowledge of the old.

**Dance:**

Dance in a circle, doing the grapevine step.( One step in front, one
step in back, see Introduction ) As you step back, honor the past;
as you step forward, honor the future.
Hold hands throughout, raising and lowering them slowly in
rhythm with the music. Think of the ebb and flow of life, of the
bonding of women in sisterhood throughout time.

# A Circle of Women

*Mary Ann Fusco © 1984*

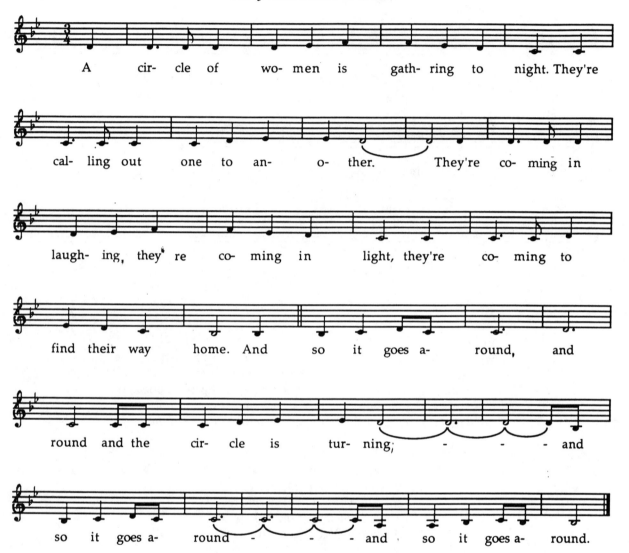

A cir- cle of wo- men is gath- ring to night. They're cal- ling out one to an- o- ther. They're co- ming in laugh- ing, they're co- ming in light, they're co- ming to find their way home. And so it goes a- round, and round and the cir- cle is tur- ning; — — and so it goes a- round — — — and so it goes a- round.

**Verses:**

A circle of women, a womb safe and warm,
where life is forever re-birthing.
The mothers and daughters, the maidens and crones,
the circle is calling them home.
And so it goes around, the circle is calling.

A circle of women is dancing tonight.
A circle of women is singing.
They're sharing the world with their wisdom and light
and their magic is taking them home.
And so it goes around, the magic is growing.

(Same as verse #1 except last line)
Their power is taking them home.
And so it goes around, the power is growing.

# Isla Mujeres

*Ann Williams*
*Recorded on* Song of the Jaguar © 1989

Mu- jer- es, I hear you cal- - ling. Muj- eres, my heart sings back to you.

Mu- jer- es, I hear you cal- - ling. Mu-jeres , my heart sings back to you.

I hear you in the wind, I feel you in the sea. I touch you in the earth, I feel you

in all things - -

**Verse:**
Grandmothers, (women, sisters, brothers, etc.) we hear you
calling.
Our heart sings back to you.
We hear you in the wind, we feel you in the sea,
we touch you on the earth, we see you in all things.

**Spanish words:**
Abuelas, oigo su canto.
Abuelas mi corazon canta a vos (todos).
Mujeres, oigo su canto
Mujeres mi corazon canta a vos.
Te escucho en el viento,
Te siento en el mar,
Te toco en la piel,
Te siento en todo.

# River of Birds

*Recorded by Libana on* A Circle is Cast, © 1986

There's a ri-ver of birds in mi- gra- tion, a

na- tion of wo- men with wings.

This chant beautifully captures the essence of sisterhood and the growing momentum of the women's spirituality movement. Add the harmony lines one by one. You can change the word 'there's' to 'we're' a river of birds.

## Woman as Life Giver
## The Universal Mother

The following chants and dances honor woman as the life giver, the universal, bountiful mother, creatress of all things.

This Peruvian Venus is Pacha Mama, the Earth Mother who provides life and sustenance for all the children of the planet.

# Ancient Mother

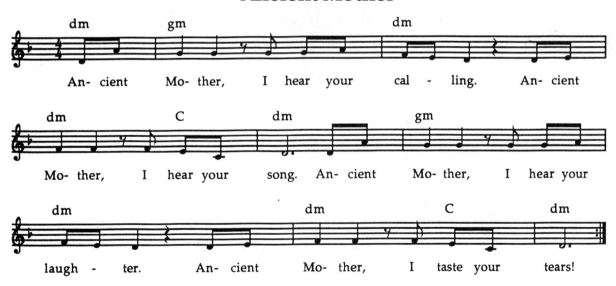

An- cient Mo- ther, I hear your cal - ling. An- cient Mo- ther, I hear your song. An- cient Mo- ther, I hear your laugh - ter. An- cient Mo- ther, I taste your tears!

**Verse: Traditional words from Africa**
O la mama wa ha su kola
O la mama wa ha su wam
O la mama kow wey ha ha ha ha
O la mama ta te kayee

# Mother of All Things

*LisaThiel*
*Recorded on* Songs of the Spirit © 1984

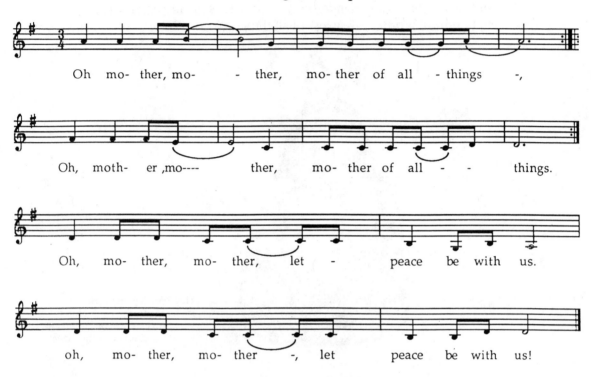

Oh mo- ther, mo- - ther, mo- ther of all -things -,

Oh, moth- er ,mo---- ther, mo- ther of all - - things.

Oh, mo- ther, mo- ther, let - peace be with us.

oh, mo- ther, mo- ther -, let peace be with us!

**Verses:** Add your own prayers such as let 'hope', 'beauty', 'wisdom', etc. be with us.

As you chant, visualize the mother in her fullness. Ask her for healing for yourself and all beings.

# Return to the Mother

Re turn to the mo - ther Re- turn to the mo - ther. Re

turn to the mo - ther, die and be re- born.

# My Divine Mother

*Paramahansa Yogananda*

En- grossed is the bee of my mind on the blue

lo- tus feet of my di- vine mo- ther. En- grossed

**2.** vine Mo- ther. Di- vine Mo- ther, my Di

vine Mo- ther. Di- vine Mo- ther, my Di- vine Mo- ther Di

**2.** **D.S.** vine Mo- ther. En- grossed.

# Take your Gifts Mother

*Priscilla Almada Branthaver and Kate Marks*

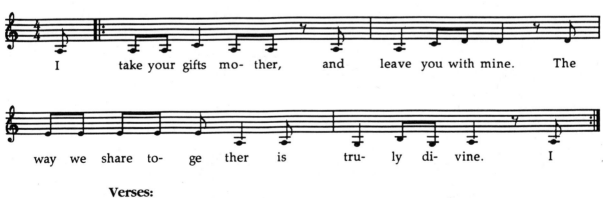

I take your gifts mo- ther, and leave you with mine. The

way we share to- ge ther is tru- ly di- vine. I

**Verses:**

| | |
|---|---|
| Spirit Goddess.......bless each other | Wisdom women.....know each other |
| Love Mother.........touch each other | Heart maiden........love each other |
| Wounds sister.......heal each other | Songs daughter......sing together |

# Sacred Corn Mother

*Lisa Thiel*
*Recorded on* Prayers for the Planet © 1984

Corn is a symbol of fertiilty among many Native peoples.

Sa- cred corn Mo- ther, co- me to me. Make my way sa- cred,

fill me with beau- ty. Fill me with beau- ty, fill me with

beau- ty, Fill me - with beau- ty, that I may bring

o - thers beau- ty.

# She is Bountiful, She is Beautiful

*Susan Arrow* © 1981
Recorded on *Welcome Sweet Pleasure*

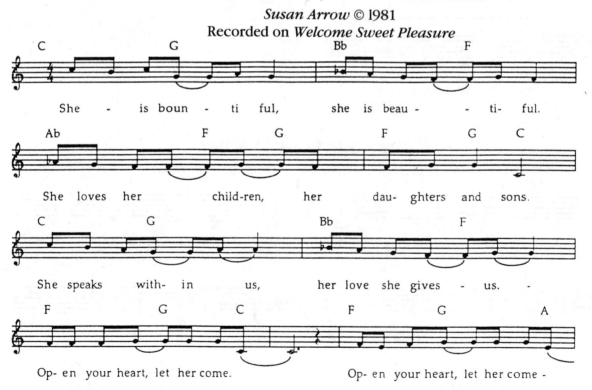

She - is boun - ti ful, she is beau - - ti - ful.

She loves her child-ren, her dau - ghters and sons.

She speaks with- in us, her love she gives - us. -

Op- en your heart, let her come. Op- en your heart, let her come -

## Woman's Blood Power

A woman's monthly blood (menstruation) is the most sacred source of her life giving power and mystery. Like a snake that regularly sheds its skin, a woman's womb sheds its lining once a month symbolizing the ever–renewing life force.

Modern women have been conditioned to hide and be ashamed of their bleeding time. In traditional cultures, women are honored at the time of their menses (also called 'moon time') They are given special rites of passage to celebrate the coming of their first blood, of their womanhood. In many Native American traditions, women retreat to special women's lodges (called moon lodges) during their moon time to meditate and cleanse. They are not expected to work, but to be open and receptive to guidance and visions that they later share with their people.

As you chant, alone or with other menstruating women, go out into nature and release your blood into the earth.

# Mine is the Blood
*Cerridwen Fallingstar*

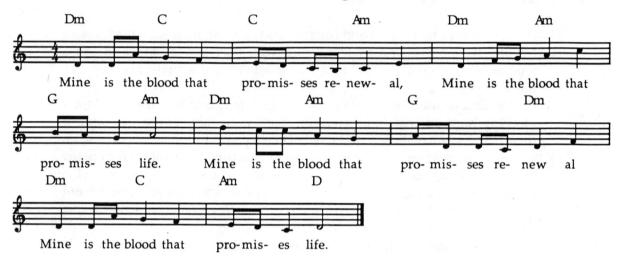

Mine is the blood that pro- mis- ses re- new- al, Mine is the blood that
pro- mis- ses life. Mine is the blood that pro- mis- ses re- new al
Mine is the blood that pro- mis- es life.

# Source to Source
*Mary Ann Fusco ©*

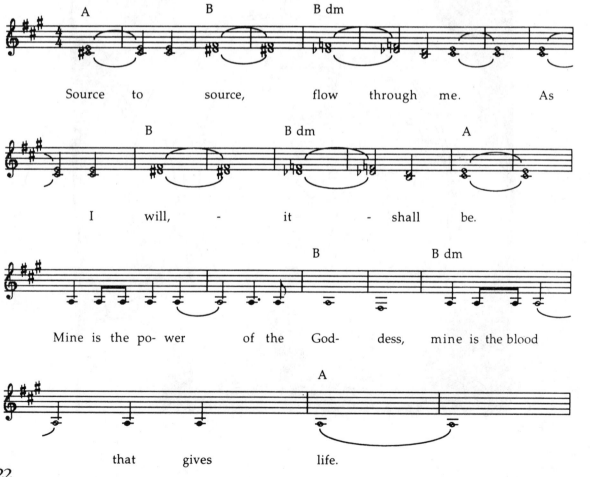

Source to source, flow through me. As
I will, - it - shall be.
Mine is the po- wer of the God- dess, mine is the blood
that gives life.

# Willow Song (Sha Noon)

*Native American—Chumash Tradition*

Sha- noon ho yah sha- Hey hey yuh hey yuh yah ho ney, Hey ney, Ho ney Ho ney

The willow tree is a symbol of female power, flexibility and strength. Its roots go deep into the earth, helping us to stay grounded, and connected to Mother Earth through the storms and stressfull times of our lives. Its branches bow and bend, giving us flexibility and the ability to flow with changes.

The chant is sung especially for girls at the time of puberty and their first bleeding to honor their growing power, strength and reciliency. Sing it three times, swaying like the willow branches and grounding your feet deep into the earth. Traditionally, the chant begins with the Ho ney, Ho ney phrase. Accompany it with a rattle only.

## Birth

The following chants honor the power of birth. Chant them at an actual birth or for an individual or collective re–birthing ceremony.

# Yani Yoni Ya Hu Way Hey

*Native American*

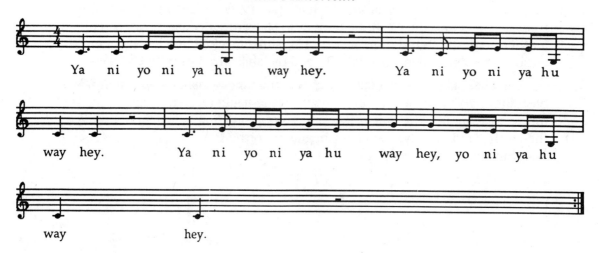

Ya ni yo ni ya hu way hey. Ya ni yo ni ya hu

way hey. Ya ni yo ni ya hu way hey, yo ni ya hu

way hey.

This birthing chant helps bring on labor, ensures easy delivery and a strong healthy baby. Chant it at the time of the new moon to bring blessings.

# Keep Breathing
*Nina Wise*

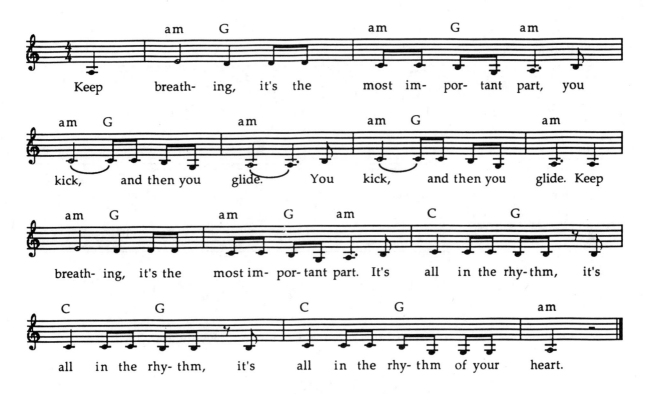

Keep breath- ing, it's the most im- por- tant part, you kick, and then you glide. You kick, and then you glide. Keep breath- ing, it's the most im- por- tant part. It's all in the rhy- thm, it's all in the rhy- thm, it's all in the rhy- thm of your heart.

This was originally a song written by a mother to help her child learn to swim. The words can be adapted for a birthing chant. **Verses:**

It kicks.....deep down inside
It kicks.....push down inside
You push...deep down inside
In 2 parts:
Part 1—Keep breathing, it's the most important part, it's all in the rhythm, its all in the rhythm, it's all in the rhythm of your heart
Part 2—You kick...etc.

# Bless The Shining Children

Bless the shi- ning child- ren our love brings to ground

# We Wish You A Happy Birthday

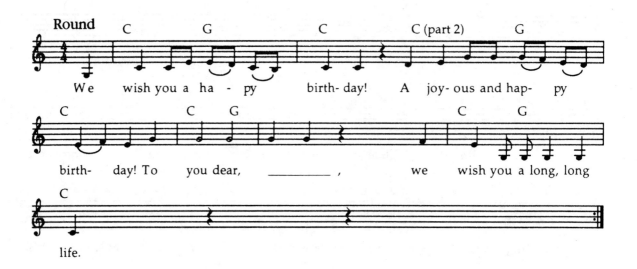

An alternative to the usual birthday song. Sing it also as a blessing for a birth.

# Man Gwa Nem

*African Lullaby*

Women throughout all times and cultures have sung their children to sleep. Lullabies help us connect with the nurturing, mothering part of ourselves.

# By A Woman

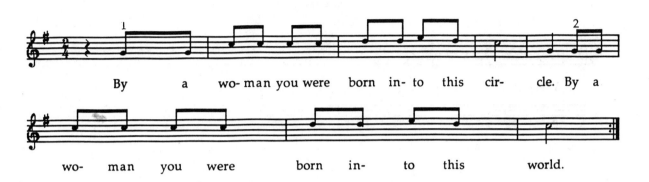

By    a   wo- man you were   born in- to  this   cir-   cle. By a

wo-   man   you   were   born  in-   to   this   world.

# You Are a Hollow Bamboo

You - are    a  hol- low bam- boo,    op-en up and let the    babe - come through.

**Verse:**
I am a hollow bamboo
Open up and let the love go through

# In Balance with the Moon

*Catherine Madsen*

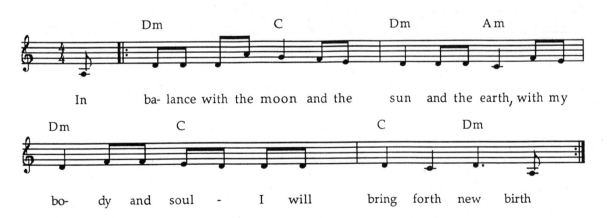

In    ba- lance with the  moon  and the    sun   and the earth, with my

bo-   dy  and  soul  -    I  will    bring  forth  new   birth

# Welcome Little One

*Starhawk*

Wel- come, lit- tle one. Wel- come, lit- tle one, we've been

wait- ting for you, we're so glad to see you

# Eni Wichi Chayo

*Native American Birth Chant*

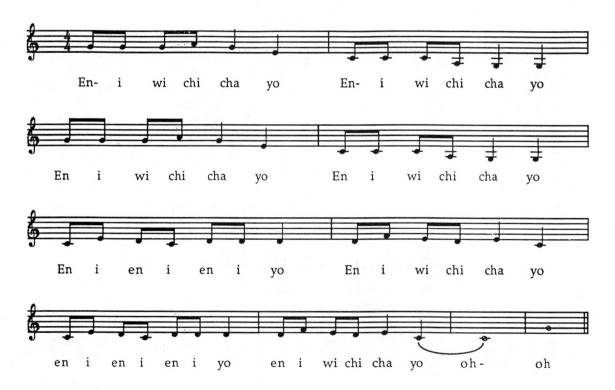

En- i wi chi cha yo En- i wi chi cha yo

En i wi chi cha yo En i wi chi cha yo

En i en i en i yo En i wi chi cha yo

en i en i en i yo en i wi chi cha yo oh- oh

The following ritual can be done to help us reconnect with our own birth. Tune into what your actual birth was like. How would you like this re-birthing experience to be different? Share your feelings with the group before you take your turn, so they can empower you.

## Re-birthing Ritual

Divide the group into partners. Clasp hands with a partner and make a bridge to represent the birth canal, a womblike tunnel. The birth canal can also be made with participants opening their legs in a long line or kneeling on all fours, alternating heads and feet.

*Each person being re-born is blindfolded and then crawls through the canal. Those who are making the canal will restrain, push, or gently touch the 'newborn' as he/she passes through. They chant his/her name and other powerful affirmations, such as 'You are special'.*

*As the newborn arrives, the blindfold is removed; He/she is hugged warmly and greeted with words such as 'We welcome you'.*

## Woman as Goddess

Most traditional cultures of the world have rich mythologies peopled with many Gods and Goddesses. By exploring these mythologies today, we can attune to different expressions of the divine.

The Goddess represents the archetype of the divine feminine. She is known by many names and forms and is closely associated with the moon.

# Opening Up

Round

I am o pe- ning up in sweet sur- ren - der to the

lu- mi- nous love- light of the God - dess;

O - pe- ning, o - pe- ning - -.

Sing each part twice. As each part is sung simultaneously, a beautiful counterpoint is created.

**Dance:**
**Part 1—I am opening up in sweet surrender**
All hold hands and move into center,
raising arms slowly.
**To the luminous love light of the goddess**
Release hands, spin out.
**Part 2—Opening, opening**
Spin slowly to the left (moonwise), right
arm/palm up, to sky, left arm/palm down, to earth, channelling
light to the earth. Keep spinning throughout.
(Also substitute the Lord, or the One instead of the Goddess)

# We All Come from the Goddess

*Z Budapest* © 1971

*Recorded on* From the Goddess, *Spring Hill Music*

We all come from the God-dess, and to her we shall re-turn, like a

drop of rai - n, flo- wing to the o - - cean.

Sing this chant unaccompanied, adding simple harmonies a third and a fifth above the melody. Or sing it as a counterpoint to *Isis, Astarte, Diana* or *The Goddess is Alive* chants described below. To balance with male energies, add the verses for *We all Come from the Sun God* in Chapter Five. You can also sing and dance it with *Hoof and Horn* (see Chapter Five) as a counterpoint.

**Dance:.** Do it in two parts, in two circles.
Circle A–Inner Circle
**1. We all come from the Goddess**
Take four steps toward center raising arms and head upward, greeting the Goddess.
**2. And to her we shall return**
Take four steps back lowering arms, feeling the presence of the Goddess returning.
3. **Like a drop of rain**
Repeat #1–facing on a slight diagonal to the right. Imagine the rain falling through your fingers.
**4. Flowing to**
As you step back make a full turn slowly to the right.
**5. the ocean.**
Lower arms down on each side and let them swing back behind you, Imagining you are opening up to an ocean wave.
Repeat this Goddess chant and dance over and over.
Circle B–Outer Circle (For this chant see Chapter Five)
1. **Hoof and Horn, Hoof and Horn**
Stand in place: Stamp each foot rhythmically with the beat of the music. Hold your index fingers up on each side of your head, symbolizing horns.
2. **All that dies**
Lower hands down slowly toward earth, palms down, lower head.
3. **Shall be re-born.**
Slowly raise hands and head up, palms facing skyward.
Repeat this God chant and dance over and over.
If you only have a small group, do the dance in one circle with all participants doing both parts consecutively.

# Children of the Goddess

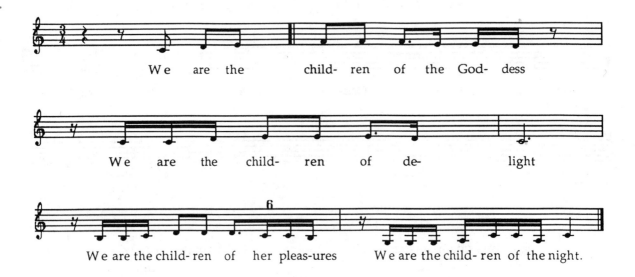

We are the     child- ren   of the God- dess

We  are  the  child- ren   of  de-     light

We are the child- ren  of  her pleas-ures     We are the child- ren of the night.

# The Goddess is Alive

*Adapted from the song 'God is Alive' by Buffy St Marie*

God-   dess    is  a- live!     Ma-  gic   is  a   foot.

This is a simple catchy chant to call in the Goddess. It can also simply be spoken. Change the first word and adapt it to many situations. For example: 'Rachel is alive.', 'Love is Alive.', 'The moon is Alive', etc. It is also a counter-point to *Isis, Astarte, Diana* or *We all Come from the Goddess*.

# Goddess of Life

*Music: Hauptmann (1792–1865) Words: M. D. Novack*

Canon in four voices

We are the chil- dren of the God- dess of Life; and we

sing and dance a- round the fi- re bright.

# Isis Astarte Diana

*Words: Deena Metzger  Music: Charlie Murphy*
*This is the chorus from a longer chant called* 'The Burning Times'
*Recorded on* Catch the Fire © 1981

I sis, As tar te, Di a na, He ca te, De me ter, Ka li,

In an na.

This chant invokes the Goddess in her many forms. It can also be sung with *We are an Old People, We all come from the Goddess, Goddess is Alive, Hoof and Horn, and Crone and Sage.* For the God verses, see *Mithra Osiris* in Chapter Five.

**Isis**—Egyptian Goddess / high priestess.
**Astarte**—Syrian fertility Goddess
**Diana**—Roman moon and nature goddess, the huntress also known as Artemis (Greek), associated with independent, strong, youthful energy.
**Hecate**—Greek moon goddess, the dark crone, associated with the underworld, magic, death and rebirth.
**Demeter**—Greek goddess of the fruitful earth, the Earth Mother who, according to the myth, stops all living things from growing and makes the earth barren for half of each year while her daughter Persephone is in the underworld.
**Kali**—Hindu Goddess associated with death. She is the destroyer but also a powerful creative force. She is often depicted as black-skinned with loose hair, wearing necklaces of skulls. On the inside she has a heart of gold and will give protection to all who know her.
**Innana**—Sumerian goddess – her name means 'lady of heaven'. In the myth about her she visits the underworld and learns about the forces of death and regeneration. She is able to master and embody the energies of light and darkness.

**Dance:** Do a basic side-step or grapevine (one step for each name) holding hands in W hold position in a circle. This dance can be done as a counterpoint to *We All Come From the Goddess* ( see chant/dance p 131 ) using a small group in the center of the circle.

# Isis, Heart of the Mountain

*Alicia Bonnet*
*Recorded on* Openings © 1982

**Verses:** add more Goddess names:

**Lilith—**considered the first wife of Adam, according to Middle Eastern myths of creation and the Talmud, holy book of the Hebrews. Genesis is said to be a patriarchal revision, suppressing memories of the primordial mother. The original version describes how both Adam and Lilith were created at the same time. Lilith refused to subordinate herself to Adam, or the male God.

**Astarte—**See previous reference.

**Gaia—**Mother of the Earth.

**Kali—**See reference on next pages.

# Alma Hina

*Mary Ann Fusco ©*

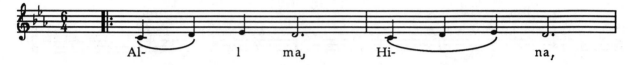

**Verse:**
Luna, Hera, Gaia.

**Alma**—Middle Eastern Temple woman, Hebrew moon Goddess
who mothered kings in a Jerusalem cult.
**Hina**—Polynesian moon goddess and creatress of the world. All
women embody her spirit. Hence 'wahine' means woman.
**Metra**—Persian name of the moon. Metra is the mother whose love
penetrates everywhere.
**Luna**—Roman moon goddess, identified with Diana. Her crazy
followers were called Lunatics.
**Hera**—Greek consort of Zeus and Queen of Olympus.
**Gaia**—Greek earth mother goddess.
**Albion**—Milk white moon goddess associated with the Milky Way.
**Fatima**—Arabian moon goddess. Her name means Creatress.
**Selene**—Greek Moon Goddess.

# Kali Durga

Ka- li Dur- - ga na mo na

ma a a a Ka- li Dur- ga

na- mo na ma a a Ka- li Dur ge

Na- mo na ma a a Ka- li Dur- ge

Na mo na ma Ka- li Dur- ga

na mo na ma ka- li dur- ge

na- mo na ma-

Kali—Hindu/Tibetan War Goddess called the Black Mother. She is known for her fierce nature, her ability to destroy as well as be a powerful creative force. She is depicted as black skinned, loose haired with many arms, carrying a sword and skulls. Durga is another aspect of the dark mother, Kali.

137

# Hindu Goddess Chant

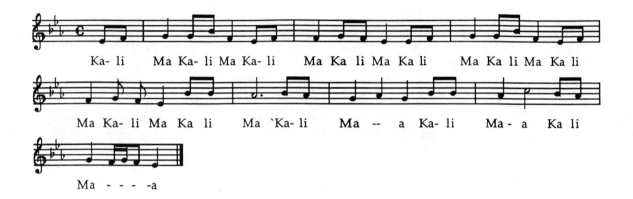

Ka- li   Ma Ka- li Ma Ka- li   Ma Ka li Ma Ka li   Ma Ka li Ma Ka li

Ma Ka- li Ma Ka li   Ma `Ka- li   Ma -- a Ka- li   Ma - a   Ka li

Ma - - - -a

A Hindu chant honoring different aspects of the Goddess/Divine Mother. Often in Hindu mythology the same Goddess can have many names or merge with other Goddesses.

**Verses:**

**Durga Ma**—Warrior Goddess. She is fierce and invincible, often depicted as a beautiful yellow woman with ten arms, standing on a lion, carrying weapons.
**Sita Ma**—Wife of Rama. She is a symbol of loyalty and selfless love.
**Rhade Ma**—A cowherd girl loved by Krishna. She represents devotion.
**Lakshmi Ma**—Goddess of wealth and fortune. Wife of Vishnu.
**Shakti Ma**—Mother Goddess, symbol of female, creative energy and fertility.
**Ganga Ma**—Goddess of the Ganges River. It is said that she carries with her all those who have died, washing away their sins.
**Parvati Ma**—Goddess of the Himalayas, consort to Shiva.
**Saraswati Ma**—Goddess of Art and Music.

# Om Tara Tu Tara

Om    Ta    ra    tu    Ta    ra    tu-    re    Swa-    ha

Invocation to the Goddess Tara, honored in the Tibetan Buddhist tradition.

# Kwan Zeon Bosai

Buddhist chant from Korea honoring Quan Yin, Goddess of compassion. The ideographs which are pronounced Kwan - Yin in mandarin Chinese are pronounced Kwan Ze-on ( Zeeon) in the Korean language. The name translates as 'She who perceives (Kwan) the sounds (on) of the world ( ze)'The meaning is 'She who witnesses the distress of beings in the world, who hears their cries and accords them mercy and compassion'. Bosai is the Korean name for Bodhisattva, the enlightened, compassionate one.

As you chant, explore different harmonies.

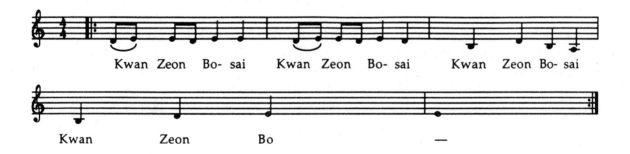

Kwan  Zeon  Bo- sai     Kwan  Zeon  Bo- sai     Kwan  Zeon  Bo- sai

Kwan        Zeon        Bo                —

# O Brighde

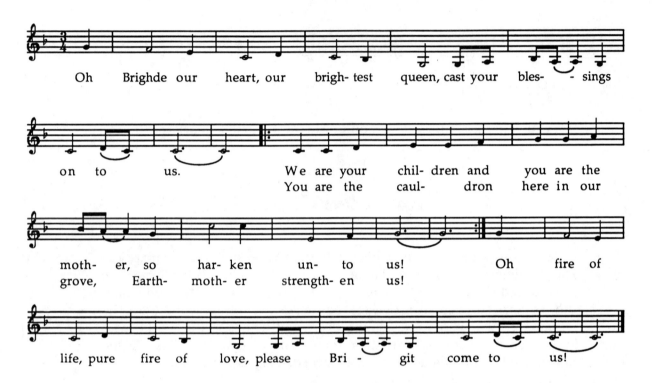

Oh Brighde our heart, our brigh- test queen, cast your bles- - sings on to us.

We are your chil- dren and you are the
You are the caul- dron here in our

moth- er, so har- ken un- to us! Oh fire of
grove, Earth- moth- er strength- en us!

life, pure fire of love, please Bri - git come to us!

A chant to honor St. Bridget (also known as Brighde, Bride, Brigid). She was worshipped and honored throughout Celtic Europe long after Christianity took hold. Most popular in Ireland, she is known as the white goddess, guardian of the home fire and hearth. In traditional ceremonies, she is portrayed wearing a crown of light (candles) on her head, representing the Eternal flame.

# Yemaya Asesu

*African Goddess Chant*

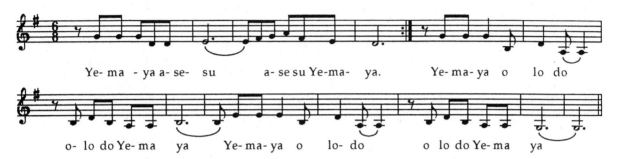

Ye- ma - ya a- se- su     a- se su Ye-ma- ya.     Ye- ma-ya  o     lo  do

o- lo do Ye- ma     ya     Ye- ma-ya  o     lo- do     o  lo do Ye- ma     ya

This chant comes from the Yoruba tradition, an earth worshipping religion from Africa. It teaches ancestor reverence and kinship between humans, plants, earth and animals.

The chant honors the energies of three Yoruba deities: Yemaya, Ochun and Oya. The following descriptions come from materials by Uzuri Amini, found in the book 'The Goddess Celebrates'. (See bibliography.)

**Yemaya**—Goddess of the Ocean. She is the giver of all life and the Great mother of us all. She provides the womb to which we can return and be reborn.

Offerings to her are cornmeal, molasses, watermelons, seashells and other things you find in the sea.

**Oya**—Goddess of the winds of change. She blows into our lives and strikes her lightening to change us. Offerings to her include red wine, eggplant and grapes.

**Oshun**—Goddess of the Oshun River. She is the river that flows around obstacles in our path. She opens our sexuality. Offerings to her are French pastries, oranges, cinnamon, pumpkins and especially honey.

**Verses:**

Oya Asesu
Asesu Oya 2x
Ochun Asesu
Asesu Oshun, etc.

# Women and the Moon

The moon, like the sun, has been honored and worshipped throughout the ages in all cultures of the world. It is associated with the Goddess, with feminine power, deep emotions, and the unconscious. The moon influences the basic rhythms of life and the flow of all water on earth—the tides, rains, floods, the circulation of blood and the sap in plants.

A woman's menstrual cycle is the same as the 28 1/2 day lunar cycle. The earliest calendars were based on the activity of the moon. As the moon magnetically pulls the earth's oceans, she also increases the vibratory rate of our physical and subtle bodies, and helps us in our spiritual work. The full moon is seen everywhere on the planet and is especially powerful to tune into for group ritual and planetary meditations.

# Neesa

*Native American - Senecca Tradition*

Nee- sa, nee- sa    nee- sa,    nee- sa, nee- sa,    nee- sa,    nee- sa, nee, sa,

nee- sa,    gai- we- o    gai- we- o.

' Neesa ' - means winter moon. ' Gaiweo ' pronounced Guy - way - yo. means creator / creation.

# The Moon is my Mistress

*Mary Ann Fusco ©*

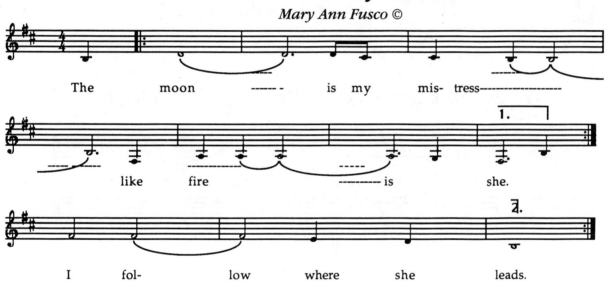

The    moon    ------ - is my    mis- tress----------------

like    fire    -------- is    she.

I    fol-    low    where    she    leads.

**Verses::**

She burns my senses
she dances on the sea
I follow where she leads.


The moon is my mother
She stills my soul
She holds me in a circle
She lets me go
I weep in her shadow
I laugh in her glow

The moon is my sister
Strong and wise
She melts the darkness
She turns the tides
I see myself in her eyes
I see myself in her eyes

## Hay Ya Hay Ya—Moon Song
*Native American Indian, Chumash tradition*

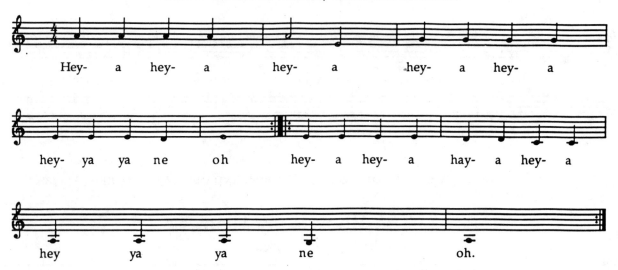

Hey- a hey- a hey- a hey- a hey- a

hey- ya ya ne oh hey- a hey- a hay- a hey- a

hey ya ya ne oh.

## We are In Tune with the Healing of the Moon

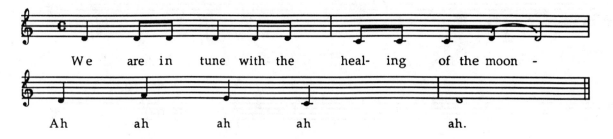

We are in tune with the heal- ing of the moon -

Ah ah ah ah ah.

This is a variation on *Come Children Come to the Radiant Sun.* It is a very catchy chant and can go on for a long time. Add harmonies and your own words such as:

**Verses:**
We are in tune with:
the Goddess in the moon, the Maiden in the moon,
the Mother in the moon,
the rising of the moon,
the waning of the moon, etc.

# Grandmother Moon

*Sage Medicine Heart*
*Recorded on* Native American Ceremonial Chants

I am wind, I am wat- er I am

mo- ther I am daught- er I am grand- mo- ther moon I am

eb- bing I am flow ing I am giv- ing, I am glow- ing I am

grand- moth- ther moon Look to the night and I'll show you my light

Look to the East for my bright- ness to rise

Look to your heart and I'll show you my part
Look to the West for the wo- man in- side

## Three Phases of the Moon—Maiden, Mother and Crone

  According to ancient women's mysteries, the phases of the moon correspond to the three cycles of womanhood–the maiden (new moon), the mother (full moon), and the crone/wise woman (the dark moon). Through these three phases, a woman experiences and honors the major passages of her life and connects more deeply with the Divine Feminine, the 'Goddess' within her. With the rise of Christianity and a patriarchal worldview, the trinity of the Maiden, Mother and Crone became supplanted by the masculine trinity of the Father, Son and Holy Spirit.

## Maiden/New Moon

The Maiden is related to the virginal phase of womahood, to purity, strength and independence. She is the young, pre-menstrual girl, as well as the strong, warrior woman, healer and priestess. She is associated with the colors white or green, the new moon, dawn and spring. We know her by many names, including Artemis, Persephone, Athena, and Diana.

The new moon is the time for new beginnings and growth; for blessing, initiating, and re-energizing creative projects.

## Maiden—New Moon Meditation

*At the time of the new moon, call on the maiden to be your guide. Allow an image of her to emerge as virgin, as independent, strong woman. Invite her to stand before you. Look at her face, her hair, her body. Spend time being with her as she takes you on a journey into her world. What can she teach you? Ask her for guidance. Receive her blessings.*

*Create a clear picture of what you want to call forth and activate at this time in your life. Hold your vision strongly and feel the energy of the new moon blessing and energizing it. Imagine yourself as a huntress, pulling back your imaginary bow. Release the arrow toward your target. Say an affirmation as you do this, such as, 'With this arrow I am now making my dreams come true'.*

# Into the Silence of the Night

*By Thunderbird Woman*
*Recorded on* The Dawning

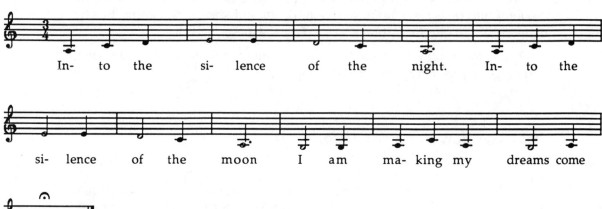

In- to the si- lence of the night. In- to the

si- lence of the moon I am ma- king my dreams come

true.

# Diana, Your Children Call

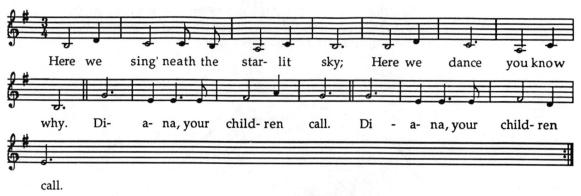

Here we sing' neath the star- lit sky; Here we dance you know

why. Di- a- na, your child- ren call. Di - a- na, your child- ren

call.

## Mother — The Full Moon

The Mother represents the fertile, reproductive, nurturing phase of womanhood. At the peak of her creative powers, she is associated with red, color of blood, with the full moon, summer and high noon. The mother is known by many names—as Demeter, Kwan Yin, Innana, Hera, Astarte, Mother Mary, Corn Mother, Levanah, Selene, and Luna.

The full moon is the time to manifest our visions and dreams, to intensify spiritual activity and expand creative work.

### Mother—Full Moon Meditation

*Imagine you are on a beach under the light of the full moon. See the moon beams shining over the water. Connect with your breath and the mysterious power of the full moon, becoming more and more receptive and open.*
*Call on the Moon Mother to be your guide. Allow an image of her to emerge. Look at her face, her hair, her body. Spend time being with her—as she takes you on a journey into her world. What does she have to teach you?*
*Feel her warm, loving arms enveloping you, nurturing and opening you. As you inhale, draw in from her the qualities you wanted from your own mother when you were a child; as you exhale, release any pains, fears or tensions you are holding. Feel her strength reaching deep inside you, reflecting the fullness and power of your own being, bringing you profound joy and peace. Receive her guidance and blessings.*

# Full Moonlight Dance

*Karen Beth, © 1977*

*Recorded on* **Each One of Us**

Under the full moon light we dance spi - rits dance we dance join-ing

hands we dance, join-ing souls re- joice.

# Moon Mother

In thy po - wer mo - ther moon, I put my faith a -

gain.

# Luna's Lullaby

*Mary Ann Fusco*
*Recorded on* Aradia's Songs For All Seasons,© 1984

Sing me a lul- la by soft and low; Moon moth- er sail- ing the

sky, sing me of ag- es gone long a- go, you who will ne- ver

die.

**Verses:**

Make me a pillow of meadowsweet
Cover my body with stars
Safe in your radiance, let me sleep
Queen of the mystic dark.

Dream me of circles and fairy rings
Whisper me secrets and charms
Wind through the willow tree, spiralling,
Gather me in your arms.

## The Crone/Dark Moon

The last phase of womanhood is represented by the old, wise, holy woman, the Crone. She is no longer physically fertile (her monthly bleeding has stopped) but is acknowledged for her spiritual fertility, her deep wisdom and knowledge. She now holds her blood, her power within her. She is the mistress of death and rebirth and a guide into the underworld; into the dark, shadow aspects of our being. She is known by many names, as Grandmother, Dark mother, Kali, Hecate, Anna, Changing Woman, Sarah or Cerridwen.

The crone is associated with black, winter and the dark moon—time for release, and regeneration.

### Crone—Dark Moon Meditation

*Find a quiet place to sit on a dark, moonless night. Go deep within; contact your fears, the shadow aspects of your being. Ask yourself what needs to be released in your life; what needs to die or be transformed within you!*

*Call on the crone to guide you. As she comes to you, notice how she looks. Study her wise old face, look deep into her penetrating eyes. Take her outstretched hands, as she leads you into the dark underworld of your psyche. Ask her for guidance and strength to help you make changes in your life. Spend time interacting with her, listening to her words of wisdom for you. Receive her blessings. When you are ready, thank her, leave her a gift, and return slowly from your journey.*

# Hecate, Cerridwen

*By Patricia Witt ©*
*Recorded on* Chants– Ritual Music, *Reclaiming Community*

This chant honors the crone in the forms of Hecate and Cerridwen.
Hecate is a Greek goddess, Queen of the night, Goddess of the dark moon.
She shared power with Zeus for many centuries. She was honored because
of her age and wisdom; some of her worshippers believe she had three
heads and could look in three directions at once—into the past, the present
and the future.

Cerridwen, from the Celtic tradition, is the Welsh dark mother, known for
for the magical power of her cauldron, source of knowledge and inspiration.

Include this chant in a ritual to call on the old wise ones, to confront death,
the dark, the shadow, the cold winter. Have one woman (the eldest, if
possible) play the part of Hecate/Cerridwen. She sits in the dark with a black
cape, cauldron and magic staff. Others in the ritual form a procession to
meet her. She gives them her blessing, a gift, and her words of wisdom.

# Crone and Sage

This is sung to the same melody as the men's chant *Hoof and Horn* in
Chapter Five. Sing it as a counterpoint to We *all Come from the Goddess.*

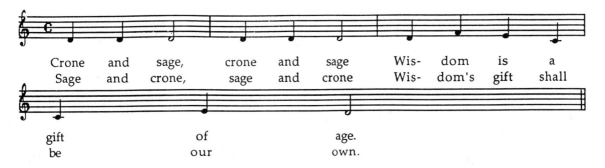

The following chants celebrate all three phases of the Goddess and the moon as maiden (new moon), mother (full moon), and crone (dark moon).

# Triple Goddess Chant

*Peter Soderberg*

**Verses:**
Holy Maiden Huntress,
Artemis, Artemis.
Maiden, come to us.
(New Moon)

Silver shining wheel
of radiance, radiance.
Mother, come to us.
(Full moon)

Ancient Queen of Wisdom,
Hecate, Hecate.
Old one, come to us.
(Dark moon)

For the verse for men, see Chapter Five.

# She's Been Waiting

*Paula Walowitz* ©

She's been wait- ing, wait- ing. She's been wait-ing so long. She's been

wait- ing for her child- ren to rem- em- ber to re- turn.

Bless- ed be, and bless- ed are, the lo -vers of the la- dy.
the ones who dance to- geth-er.

**1.**

Bles- sed be and bles- ed are the mo- thers, maid- ens, crones.

ones who dance a- lone

**Verses:**

Blessed be and blessed are: the ones who work in silence
the ones who shout and scream
the movers and the shakers
the dreamers and the dream.

# Mother, Maiden, Crone in Me
*Shekhinah Mountainwater*

# Mother Goddess Keep Me Whole
*Shekhinah Mountainwater*

**Verses:**
Maiden Goddess, let thy Beauty fill my soul.
Mother Goddess, let thy Power fill my soul.
Crone Goddess, let thy Wisdom fill my soul.

**Dance:**
Create an improvised dance expressing the three phases of womanhood and how they are expressed within you

• Begin a dance/song to express the maiden within you. When you feel complete, move slowly into stillness. Then let the dance/song of your mother aspect emerge till this feels complete. Return to stillness and finally let your crone song/dance emerge.

• After dancing each one seperately, create a dance where all three aspects are intermingling, moving within you simultaneously. Allow a dialogue to occur between the different aspects. Which aspect is most dominant? Take as long as you wish to complete your dance.

# Chapter Five

# Male Power

# Male Power

## Meditation—Male Power

*Imagine yourself in a landscape which represents the masculine aspect of your being. Allow images to emerge that are connected with your male power. What are the dominant colors, elements, sounds, smells, and shapes? Perhaps you find a bright sun shining, tall fir trees, and high mountain peaks. Notice what plants, animals and stones are there. Take time to explore this landscape, bringing in rich detail, opening all your senses. On your journey, discover a fire burning and a circle of men chanting, and drumming around it. There are men of all ages and colors. Move toward the fire, feel its light and warmth purifying and energizing you. Look into the faces of the men in the circle. They are the faces of your male ancestors; of men you have known; of powerful, wise men; of heroes, and Gods. Take time to be with them and share in any way that you wish.*

*Then, focus on a specific man who represents an ideal for you. Invite him to stand before you. Let your eyes meet. Interact with him as long as you wish. Ask him what you need at this time for your growth, and to come more fully into your masculine power. Receive his blessings and guidance.*

*Look inside yourself for the energy that represents your inner masculine power. You may perceive it as an actual being, or a symbol. Begin to embody and express this masculine energy, allowing sound and movement to emerge. What messages and teachings do you receive as you explore your inner masculine?*

## Celebrating Male Power

The women's spirituality movement, maturing over the last twenty five years, has been challenging our male dominated society, and men in particular, to break out of centuries of patriarchal conditioning. As a result, more and more men today are gathering in support groups, searching for gentler, more authentic and balanced ways to express their masculinity. They are learning to open their hearts, express emotions, and embrace the feminine, intuitive aspects of their being. As they begin to re-define who they are, they are exploring different masculine archetypes and roles—such as father, son, husband, warrior, hero, king, wild man, and shaman/priest. They are discovering new Gods and myths, reclaiming their own male mysteries and ancient heritage of worship to nature and the Goddess.

The men's liberation/spirituality movement is still very new. There are few songs and chants to reflect the changing male consciousness, especially as compared to those for women . For example, there is a need for more chants and songs about father / son relationships and brotherhood. Many of the ones shared in this first section derive from other chants or serve as counterpoints to women 's chants. As we attune to the divine masculine, we need to find / create sacred music for men which reflects our changing time and honors men's unique gifts. (Ed. note: Men are enouraged to record their own chants, dances, and rituals and send them to me so we can expand this chapter in future editions)

The following chants, drawn mostly from the contemporary Pagan and men's spirituality movements, celebrate male power. They help us, whether we are men or women, to explore different masculine archetypes and expressions of God and come into balance and inner harmony.

# Male I Am

*Music -Andreas Corbin ( See Air I Am in Chapter Two)*
*Words by Shan, House of the Goddess with additions by Kate Marks*

Create your own verses as you do a power dance in the center of a circle. Substitute individual men's names such as 'Man I am, Tom I am ' etc

**Verses:**
Male I am, Spirit I am
Priest of all the earth I am

Male I am, desire I am
Tender sweet and fierce I am

Male I am, harvest I am
Sacrifice and king I am

Male I am, strength I am
Father, son, and provider I am

Male I am, guardian I am
Warrior, and fighter I am

Male I am, open I am
Baby in her arms I am

Today, in drumming circles and councils, men are re-connecting with their instinctual, wild man/animal nature; exploring the time before the rise of patriarchy when their spirituality was centered around nature, the Goddess, fertility and the hunt. They are learning about earlier traditional societies where men felt close to the animals they hunted, frequently imitating and honoring them in their ceremonies. In these societies, the idealized Gods were often portrayed as half man/half animal.

One popular form of the animal God archetype is the horned God, who was worshipped along side the Goddess in Celtic Europe. The horns represent fertility as well as the crescent moon. Many of the horned animals—such as the buffalo, elk and bull are considered sacred. Unfortunately, with the rise of Christianity, and the repression of our wilder instincts, the image of the horned God was distorted into that of the Devil.

# Horned One, Lover, Son

*By Buffalo*
*Recorded on* Welcome to Annwfn © *Forever Forests*, 1986

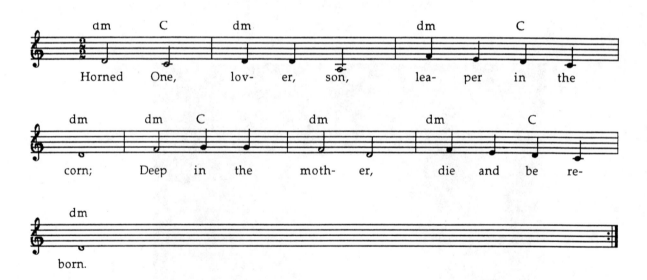

Horned One, lov-er, son, lea-per in the corn; Deep in the moth-er, die and be re-born.

# Herne

*Circle in the Greenwood*, 1990
*Recorded on* All Beings of the Earth, *Earthspirit Community*

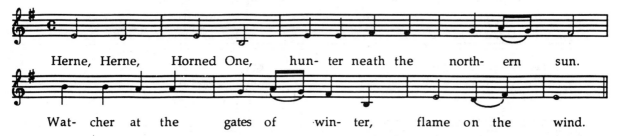

Herne, Herne, Horned One, hun- ter neath the north- ern sun.

Wat- cher at the gates of win- ter, flame on the wind.

Herne is an aspect of the horned God

# Cernunnos

*Dreow Benne*
*Recorded on* Eye of the Aeon © 1990

Cernunnos is a popular forms of the horned God. associated with the stag.

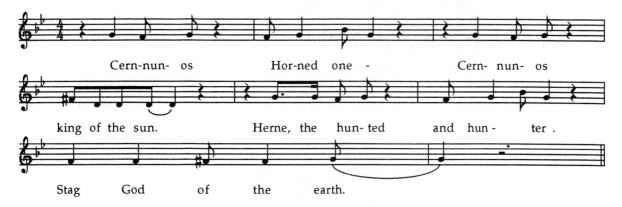

Cern-nun- os Hor-ned one - Cern- nun- os

king of the sun. Herne, the hun- ted and hun- ter .

Stag God of the earth.

### Wild Man Meditation

*Allow an inner landscape to emerge which represents the wild part of your being. Notice all the details of this wild landscape. There may be animals and other life forms there.*

*Become aware of the presence of a wild man who lives deep in a cave. Explore the cave and look closely at the wild man who represents the wild man in you. Notice his face, body, and clothing, if any. He may appear strong, hairy, and virile, or more weak and sickly. Perhaps he is half man, half animal. Begin to interact with him. What, if anything can you share or learn from each other? What qualities does he have which can be empowering for you? How can you begin to embody these? Take as long as you need to be with this wild being, opening to his teachings for you.*

# Hoof and Horn

*Ian Corrigan*

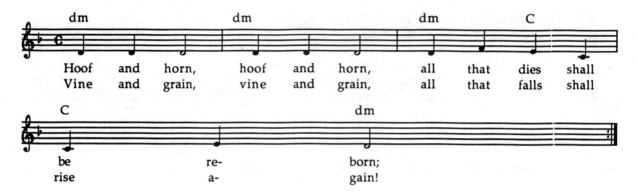

Hoof and horn, hoof and horn, all that dies shall be re- born;

Vine and grain, vine and grain, all that falls shall rise a- gain!

**Dance:**

**1. Hoof and Horn, Hoof and Horn**

Stand in place: Stamp each foot rhythmically with the beat of the music. Hold your middle fingers up on each side of your head, symbolizing horns. (For second verse—make fists instead of horns.)

**2. All that dies**

Lower hands down slowly toward earth, palms down, lower head

**3. Shall be re-born.**

Slowly raise hands and head up, palms facing skyward.

Repeat this God chant and dance over and over.

Sing and dance this as a counterpoint to *We All Come From the Goddess*. (See 'Female Power' Chapter Four) or with any of the following three God Chants.

The next three chants can be used with *Hoof and Horn* as a counterpoint as well as being sung singly, together, or as a balance to the corresponding women's chants in Chapter Four. They interweave and work well with each other. They invoke different Gods and masculine archetypes, such as the wild man, the magician, the Sun God, the king, priest and shaman. The accompanying dances can also be used singly or together. Create separate circles for each chant.

# Mithra Osiris

*Words by Shadow*

This has the same melody as *Isis Astarte* in Chapter Four. Add your own God names.

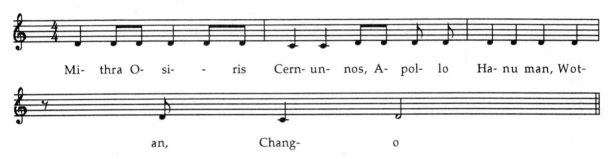

**Verses**
**Variation:** Odin, Cernunnos, Merlin, Coyote, Osiris, Shiva, Horned One
**Mithra**—The Mesopotamian horned God, represented as a bull
**Osiris**—Egyptian God
**Cernunnos**—Celtic horned Sun God
**Apollo**—Greek Sun God
**Hanuman**—Hindu Monkey God
**Wotan**—Germanic God
**Chango**—African God
**Merlin**—Celtic Magician and sage
**Odin**—Nordic God
**Coyote**—Native American—known as the shaman/trickster, master of illusions
**Pan**—Greek God; Pan means 'all'. He is part goat and part man and helps us connect with nature.

# Pan, Wotan, Baphomet

Pan, Wo- tan, Baph- o- met, Cer- nu- nos O si - ris

**Dance:**

For *Mithra Osiris* and this chant, do a rhythmic side step (or grandmother step) in a circle going sunwise, one step for each beat. Hold hands to each side of head, palms facing into circle, fingers pointing skyward, eyes straight ahead. Use this dance as a counterpoint to the chant below.

# We All Come From The Sun God

Melody is the same as *We All Come from the Goddess* in Chapter Four. Sing as counterpoint to the previous three chants.

We all come from the sun God. And to Him we shall re-turn like a

ray of light re- turn- ing to the source.

**Verse:**

We all come from the Sun God
And to him we shall return
Like a spark of flame
Rising to the heavens

**Dance:**

**1. We all come from the Sun God**—Take four steps into center raising arms up slowly toward sun

**2. And to him we shall return**—Take four steps back lowering arms slowly, forming a large crescent as if holding the sun.

**3. Like a ray of light**—Take one step to left, then one to the right facing into circle, straighten arms up toward sky like a ray of light.

**4. Returning to the source**—Spin in place, bringing hands down crossed over heart, drawing the sun energy into you.
Second time: #1 and #2 are the same.

**5. Like a spark of flame**—Take two steps to R, stamping R foot on words *spark* and *flame*. Clap hands percussively each time you stamp.

**6. Rising to the heavens.**—After second clap, hold hands together, gradually raising them toward heavens.

Another archetype closely related to the horned God is the Green Man, associated with green life, plants, forests, vegetation, and fertility. In wood carvings, he is often portrayed as grinning, with vines growing out of his mouth. Robin Hood, Jack in the Beanstalk and Pan are examples of Green Man myths which have survived as folk legends.

# Green God

*Donald Engstrom*

Green God, grass God liv- ing God of the gard- en

Hey ho hey- ho come un- to us.

**Verses:**

Sing as call and response. Change 2nd and 3rd lines.
Make up your own verses. (You can also adapt it for the Goddess.)

Rose God
Of the blossoms

Lily God
Of the waters

Planting God
Of the earth

Mushroom God
Of the fungi

Old God
 of the deep wood

# Quetzalcoatl

*Jim Berenholtz*

*Recorded on* Turquoise Waters ©1986

This chant honors Quetzalkoatl the ancient Mayan Priest King considered a powerful shaman/magician. He is associated with the feathered serpent. Temples in his honor were built in Yucatan and Palenque, Mexico.

The morn- ing star Ana-

Quetz-al co- a, Quetz-al co a tl Quetz- al co- a Quetz-al co-a

Fine

hu- ak - He

tl Quetz-al co- a Quetz- al co- a tl. Quetz-al

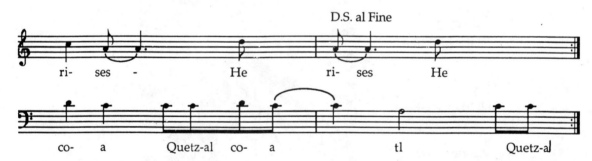

D.S. al Fine

ri- ses - He ri- ses He

co- a Quetz-al co- a tl Quetz-al

Translation: Anahuak is the ancient name of the continent of North America including Mexico and Central America.

**Verses:** Sing each of these lines as a counterpoint to the chanting of Quetzalcoatl's name.

He rises early with the dawn
He spreads his plumes around the earth
He sends his prayers skyward and in
He shines his light beside the moon

# Thoth, Hermes, Mercury

*By Abbi Spinner and J. Magnus McBride*
*Recorded on* Spinner and Magnus—Songs from the Center of the
Sacred Circle © 1993

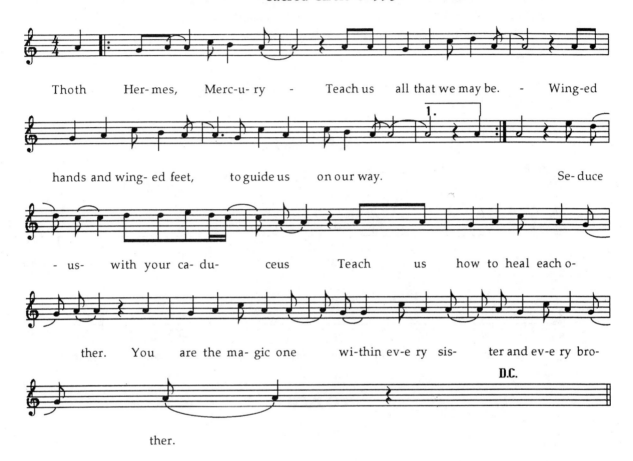

Thoth  Her- mes,  Merc-u- ry  -  Teach us  all that we may be.  - Wing-ed

hands and wing- ed feet,  to guide us  on our way.  Se- duce

- us-  with your ca- du-  ceus  Teach  us  how to heal each o-

ther.  You  are the ma- gic one  wi-thin ev-e ry sis-  ter and ev-e ry bro-

ther.

# ----------- Come to Us

Sing to the same melody as *The Triple Goddess* in Chapter Four. Feel
free to create your own verses calling forth different masculine archetypes.

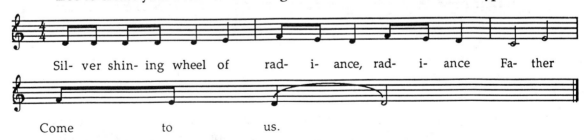

Sil- ver shin- ing wheel of  rad-  i- ance, rad-  i- ance  Fa-  ther

Come  to  us.

**Verses:** ( These words come from Shan, House of the Goddess )
Master of Wisdom
Merlin, Merlin
Magician! Come to Us

Power of the People
Arthur. Arthur
Firelord ! Come to us

169

## The Divine Masculine in the Major Religions

We are most familiar with expressions of God and the Divine Masculine as He is worshipped throughout the world in the major religions. He is Rama, Krishna, Shiva, Buddha, Jesus, Mohammed etc. The following chants honor His name in different traditions.

### Hindu

The Hindu religion has a large pantheon of Gods and a rich tradition of chanting devotional songs and mantras.

## Sri Ram

Ram is a Hindu God known for his kingly, warrior nature.

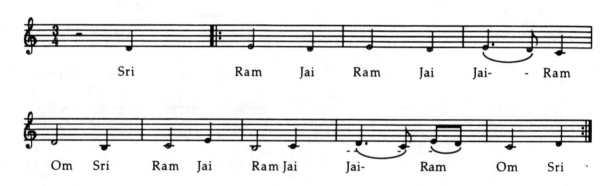

Sri    Ram    Jai    Ram    Jai    Jai- - Ram

Om    Sri    Ram    Jai    Ram Jai    Jai-    Ram    Om    Sri

## Hare Krishna

Ha- re    Krish- na, Ha- re    Krish- na, Krish- na    Krish- na, Ha- re

Ha- re. Ha- re    Ra- ma Ha- re,    Ra- ma,    Ra- ma,    Ra- ma, Ha- re    Ha- re

This chant honors two aspects of the male spirit, Krishna and Rama. Rama, described above, is the warrior. Krishna is the Divine Lover who is childlike, free and loves nature. Known for his devotion, he is usually depicted playing his flute, dancing with young maidens, and herding goats

# Gopala

Gopala is another name for Krishna; Devaki was Krishna's mother.

Go - pa- la -,  Go -pa- la -  De - va-ki nan da na  Go - pa - la

De- va- ki nan da na  Go- pa - la  De-va-ki Nan da na Go-pa- la

# Om Nama Shivaya #1

Shiva is a Hindu God who represents the masculine force in the universe, the cosmic dancer. He is the Lord of change, destroyer and transformer and helps us cut away illusion and confront our shadow aspects. As you chant to Shiva, call for change, for death of the old, birth of the new.

Om  Na ma ha Shi vai  Om  Na ma ha Shi vai Om

Na ma ha  Shivai Nam ah  Om  Om  Na ma ha Shi vai,  Om

Na ma ha Shivai  Om  Na ma ha Shivai  Nam ah  Om.

**Dance: Repeat each part twice.**

**Part 1**—Side-step rhythmically, with strength, in a clockwise direction around the circle, holding R arm/hand high above head up, fingers together pointing skyward, palm facing into circle. This hand position represents Shiva holding his trident. L hand is held down on left side, fingers pointing down to earth.

**Part 2**—Make a Shiva mudra (see diagram) with your hands. Connect your thumb and index fingers making a circle. Keep other three fingers straight. Hold this Shiva Mudra over your solar plexus, center of personal power and over the top of crown, center of spiritual power. Spin slowly alone first one way; then reverse hand positions and turn in the opposite direction. Feel the transforming power of Shiva move through you.

# Om Nama Shivaya #2

O            m      Na   ma      Shi- va            ya.

# Look into the Fire

*Suma and Tony Wrench*
*Recorded by Prana on* Second Chants © 1983

Look in- to the   fi- re,   om   na ma ha   shi   va - ya, let   go of all de-

si- re, om   na ma ha shi   va ya.   Love will get you   high - er,   learn to be a

fly- er and fly   high- er   and   high- er,   om   na ma ha shi   vay - a.

# Shiva Dance Dance Dance

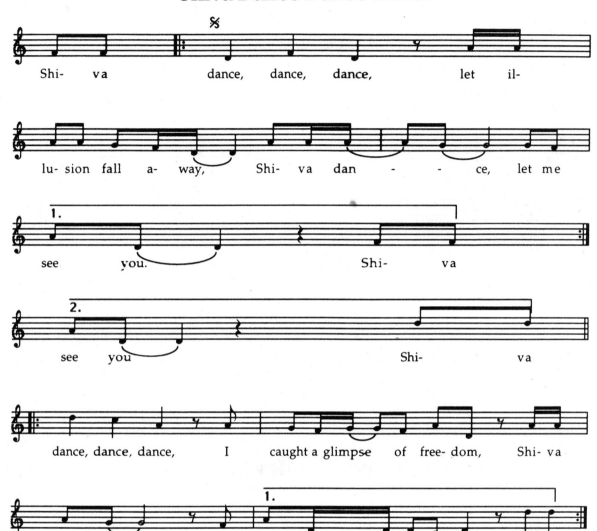

Shi- va dance, dance, dance, let il-

lu- sion fall a- way, Shi- va dan - - ce, let me

**1.** see you. Shi- va

**2.** see you Shi- va

dance, dance, dance, I caught a glimpse of free- dom, Shi- va

**1.** da - ance, I caught a glimpse of peace. Shi -va

**D.S.** al fine

caught a glimpse of peace. Shi- va

**Dance:**

**Part 1**—Up to 'Let me see you'. All dance holding hands in a circle, walking rhythmically.

**Part 2**—Spin alone and make a Shiva mudra with hands. Hold R hand high behind head, fingers pointing skyward; hold L hand down, fingers pointing to earth. Spin to the right. On last phrase, switch hands so the L is above and R is down; spin in opposite direction.

**With a partner**—Hold left hands with partner and raise R hands high behind head in Shiva mudra. Spin around together in same direction throughout, keeping eye contact.

173

# Jai Ganesh

Ganesh is the elephant deity who is guardian and protector. He helps us to overcome obstacles. He is known as the Lord of the Mind, of Supreme Wisdom.

# Om Namo Gurudev Namo

This chant honors the Guru, spiritual teacher and master.

# Ek Ong Kar

This chant, from the Sikh tradition, honors God as Guru. It translates as
'There is but one God–Truth is his name. Great is his indescribable Wisdom.'

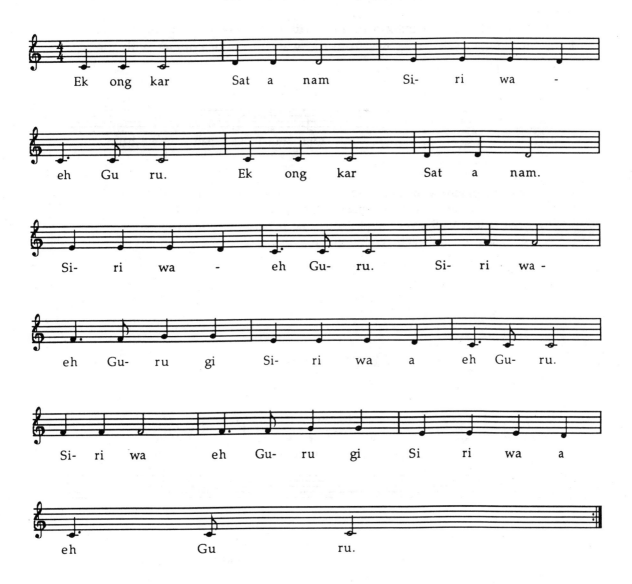

## Buddhist

Buddha is known for his wisdom, compassion and clear mind. As you chant, call on the spirit of Buddha to guide you.

# Om Mane Padme Hum

This sacred Buddhist mantra means ' hail to the jewel in the lotus.' The lotus represents purity; it grows from the water without contact with the earth

### Dance
Sing the phrase with your hands cupped in front of your heart, as if holding the jeweled lotus Concentrate on purifying your heart, your being. Walk slowly and lightly one behind the other (one step forward for each repetition) in a circle.

# Gate, Gate

This Buddhist mantra means 'Gone gone far beyond the wisdom is'. As you chant, focus on your third eye center (point between eyebrows), on the clear consciousness and detachment of Buddha.

# Padma Sambava Mantra

This Tibetan Buddhist mantra honors Padma Sambava, considered an enlightened being, a Boddhisatva.

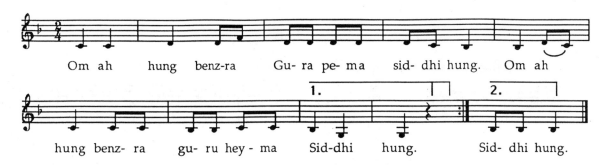

Om ah hung benz-ra Gu- ra pe- ma sid- dhi hung. Om ah

1.
2.

hung benz- ra gu- ru hey - ma Sid-dhi hung. Sid- dhi hung.

# Buddham, Saranam, Gaccami

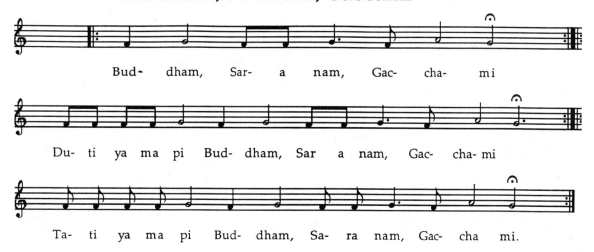

Bud- dham, Sar- a nam, Gac- cha- mi

Du- ti ya ma pi Bud- dham, Sar a nam, Gac- cha- mi

Ta- ti ya ma pi Bud- dham, Sa- ra nam, Gac- cha mi.

**Verse**:
Substitute for Buddham:
2. Dharma
3. Sangham
This prayer means:
I take refuge in the Buddha—symbol of wisdom and enlightenment.
I take refuge in the Dharma—law of cause and effect/karma
I take refuge in the Sangha—Spiritual Community
Dutiyama—a second time, Tatiyama—a third time.

## Christian

The following chants celebrate Jesus Christ in many aspects. As you chant call on Jesus to guide you and open you to expanded Christ consciousness.

# Jubilate Deo

Round of up to six parts. Come in at each measure.

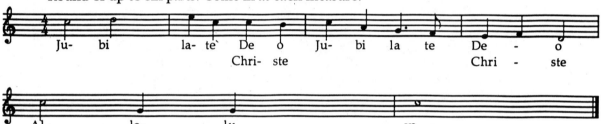

Ju- bi la- te` De o Ju- bi la te De - o
Chri- ste Chri - ste

Al- le- lu ya

**Verses:**
For calling in the Sun:

See the sun arising 2x
Darkness is gone

# Jesus Loves the Little Children

*George F. Root*

Je- sus loves the lit- tle chil- dren, all the chil- dren of the world. Red and

yel- low, black and white, they are pre- cious in His sight. Jes- us loves the lit- tle

chil- dren of the world.

Add names such as Buddha, Shiva, Krishna etc.

# Surrexit Christe

Sing very rhythmically with great joy.

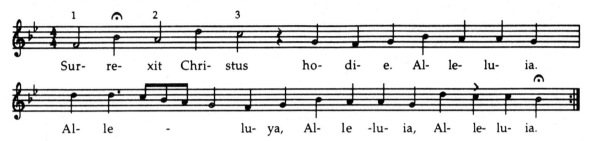

Sur- re- xit Chri- stus ho- di- e. Al- le- lu- ia.

Al- le - lu- ya, Al- le -lu- ia, Al- le- lu- ia.

**Verse**: The Christ is risen on this day (Alternate this line with
Surrext Christe hodie)

This Easter canon invokes the resurrection and re-birth of the Christ Consciousness within us all. Sing it to call in light and hope after times of darkness and despair.

# Kyrie

*Surinam*

Three part canon

Ky- ri- e, ky- ri- e. e- lei - son.

Ky- ri- e, ky- ri- e, e- lei - son.

Ky- ri- e, ky- ri- e, e- lei- son.

**Verse:** Christe Eleison

Translates as ' God have mercy. Christ have mercy '. As you chant, call on the spirit of Christ to help you forgive yourself and others.

# Lord of the Dance

*Words: Sydney Carter Music: Shaker Hymn*

I - danced on the day - when the `world was beg- un. I danced

in the moon and the stars and the sun. I danced in the hea- vens and

I came down to earth in Beth- le hem I - gave - my - birth.

Dance, dance where ev- er you may be for - I am the Lord of the

dance said - he and I will lead you all - where ev- er you may be.

I'll lead you all in the dance, said He.

**Verses:**
I danced for the scribe and the pharisee
But they wouldn't dance and they wouldn't follow me.
I danced for the fishermen James and John
They came with me and the Dance went on.
**Chorus**
It was on the Sabbath that I cured the lame
The 'holy' people said it was a shame.
So they stripped and they whipped and they hung me on high
And left me there on the cross to die.
**Chorus**

It was on a Friday that the sky turned black.
You know it's hard to dance with the devil on your back.
I leapt from my body and flew on high,
For I am the dance that can never die.
**Chorus**
They buried my body and taught that I had gone,
But I am the dance that goes on and on.
And I'll live in you if you will live in me,
For I am the Lord of the dance said he.

# Te Ariki
*Maori Hymn*

Translation: 'Christ listen to our words, listen to our hearts. We are your children. Hear our prayer in the Name of the Father, Son and Holy Spirit.'

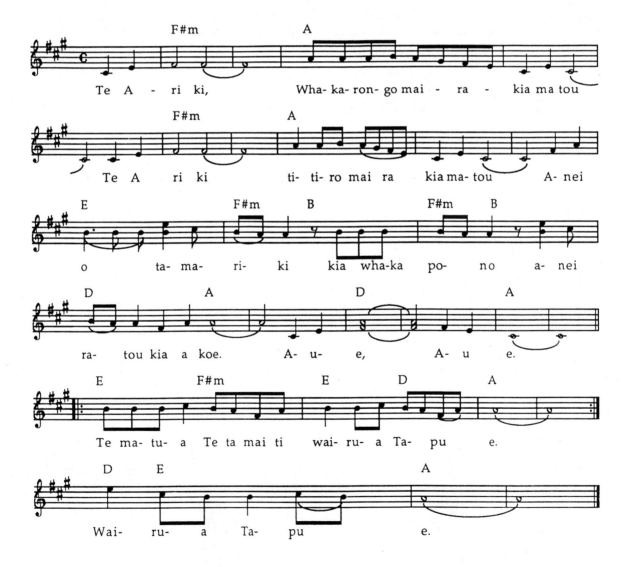

# Prayer of St. Francis

*Words: From the Prayer of St. Francis. Music: By Michael Stillwater©*
*Inner Harmony Music, 1988*

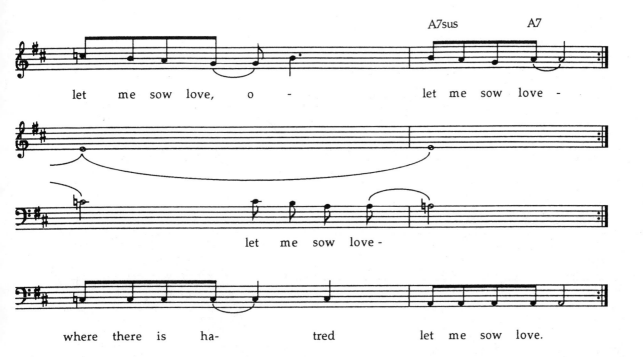

let   me   sow   love,   o -          let   me   sow   love -

let   me   sow   love -

where   there   is   ha-      tred      let   me   sow   love.

**Jewish**

# Ano Ki Shemain

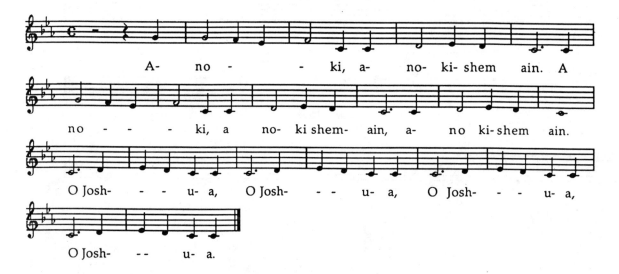

A- no - - ki, a- no- ki- shem ain. A no - - ki, a no- ki shem- ain, a- no ki-shem ain. O Josh- - - u- a, O Josh- - u- a, O Josh- - - u- a, O Josh- - u- a.

This chant helps us to attune to different Hebrew prophets and teachers Add names such as Abraham, Jacob, Moses, Solomon, etc.

# Eliyahu

This chant honors Eliya, hailed as the Messiah by the Hebrews. It is sung at Passover, when the doors are left open for him to enter.

E- li ya hu Ha na vi, E- li ya hu Ha- tish bi El i ya hu, El i ya hu, El i ya - hu, Ha gil a di, El i ya hu, El i ya hu, El i ya - hu, Ha gil a di.

**Moslem / Islamic**

# Wazifa Canon

*Words: Ancient Arabic Mantras  Arrangement :W.A. Mathieu*

Four part round

La il- la ha  il - Al- lah hu  La il- la ha  il - Al- lah hu.

Ishk Al- lah mahe  bood lil- lah.  Ishk Al- lah mahe  bood li- lah.

Ya Rah man  —  Ya - Ra - heem  il - Al- lah hu

Sub- han Al- lah Al-  ham- du- li- lah Al  lah ho  Ak- bar  Al-  lah ho

Ak-  bar  Al-  ah ho  Ak-  bar.

A Wazifa is an Arabic mantra / Sacred phrase.

The first wazifa – **La Ilaha il allah hu**— is the most holy sacred phrase in the Moslem religion. It is a prayer of rememberance. Sing the chant (first line) in unison as many times as desired; then the leader cues in the groups at two bar intervals to sing the round once through. Everybody returns to the chant and starts all over again.

## Chant:

**La Ilaha il allah hu** –There is no reality but God/ Allah

## Round:

**Ishk Allah Maheboood Lillah**–God (Allah) is love, lover and beloved

**Ya Rahman, Ya Raheem**–O Compassionate, O merciful God

**Subhan Allah** –God is pure  **Ahamdullilah** – All Praise to God

**Allah Ho Akbar**– There is no power save in Allah

These sacred phrases can also be chanted (intoned) individually as a meditiative practice.

# Ikhlas Sura

*Holy Song from the Koran (Sura 112)*

**Translation**:
Say, He is Allah
The One, the Eternal
He is neither born nor gives birth
And there is none like unto Him

# La Ilaha il Allah Hu

*Words: Traditional    Music: Kate Marks*

## Zoroastrian

The Zoroastrian religion is very ancient and predates the Judeo—Christian and Islamic traditions. Known today as the Parsees, these followers of Zoroaster worship the power of nature, the four elements and especially of light (the sun ). The mantra is the Zoroastrian name for God, God of light.

## Ahura Mazda

The following chants celebrate God in many forms.

# Twameva Maata

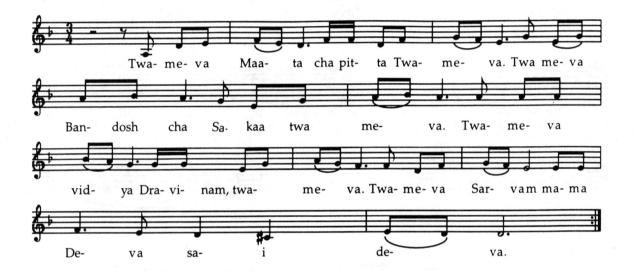

Twa- me- va   Maa-   ta cha pit-   ta Twa- me-   va. Twa me- va

Ban- dosh   cha   Sa- kaa   twa   me-   va.   Twa- me- va

vid-   ya Dra- vi-   nam, twa-   me-   va. Twa- me- va   Sar-   vam ma- ma

De-   va   sa-   i   de-   va.

This chant is often sung as part of an Arti ceremony, offering
light to the Guru/ God.

Translation:
O Lord! You are my mother, You are my father
You are my kinsman, you are my friend.
You are my knowledge and wisdom
You are my wealth of strength, valor and power,
You are my All, my God of Gods

# All I Really Want

*David Casselman © 1981*

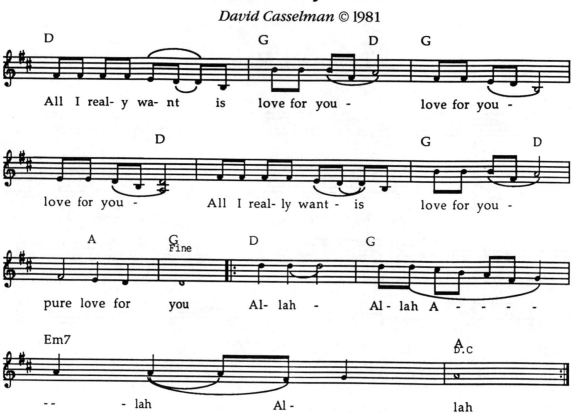

Add names such as Buddha, Shiva, Krishna etc.

# O God Beautiful

*Paramahansa Yogananda*

## Brotherhood

# En Lak' Ech /A Lak'en

*Recorded on* Gateways *by Jonathan Goldman, Spirit Sounds,* 1991

This men's chant from the Mayan tradition celebrates brotherhood. Two men and their tribes find each other in the jungle and greet each other. 'I am another you. You are another me.' It is done as a call and a response.

# Fellowship

Round

# Chapter Six

# Healing and Love

# Healing and Love

## Healing Meditation

*Sit quietly in a peaceful healing environment. Take a moment to reflect on times of major transformation in your life. How have you grown from them? Consider the suffering, the losses you have endured. What have been your most painful experiences and what have you learned from them? What do you need at this time to come into wholeness and balance? Allow an image to emerge which represents this healing for you. As you exhale, let go of any tensions and pain you are holding. As you inhale, feel healing power moving through your body, filling every cell, deeply harmonizing your being.*

## The Power of Healing

The chants and dances in this chapter help us confront our pain, connect with the innocence of our inner child and give and receive healing. Love is the most powerful healing force in the universe. As we learn to love unconditionally and to accept and forgive each other, we can heal deep wounds and transform our lives.

The following suggestions will help you create an appropriate healing ritual context for yourself and others.

### Healing Ceremony

*Send healing to yourself. Put your hands on a part of your body that needs healing, as you visualize light penetrating every cell.*

*Send healing to another. Invite them into the center of a circle (or stand opposite them). Feel yourself connected to an unlimited source of love and healing as you direct energy to them through your hands and voice.*

*Call to mind a person (or persons) with whom you wish to heal a relationship. As you chant, imagine them standing before you. Visualize the light encircling you both, clearing and harmonizing the energy between you.*

# Everything Hurt is Healed Again

*Starhawk*
*Recorded on* Chants–Ritual Music, *Reclaiming Community*

E- very-thing hurt is    healed a- gain in a    new time,    in a    new - day.

Ev- ery- thing lost is    found a- gain in a    new form in a    new    way.

This is part of *Kore's Chant* (See Chapter Four) but can be sung alone as a healing chant.

## Wash Away My Tears

*Suma*

*Recorded  by Prana on* Return of the Mayflower 1987/88

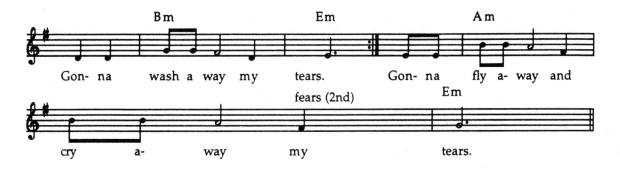

## When I Let Go of Fear

*Words: The Course in Miracles   Music : Michael Stillwater*

## Purify and Heal Us

*Adele Getty*

This simple chant can be sung for hours as part of healing ceremony. It puts us into an altered state quickly. Do it with a drumbeat and add harmonies.

# I Am A Circle, I am Healing You

*Adele Getty*

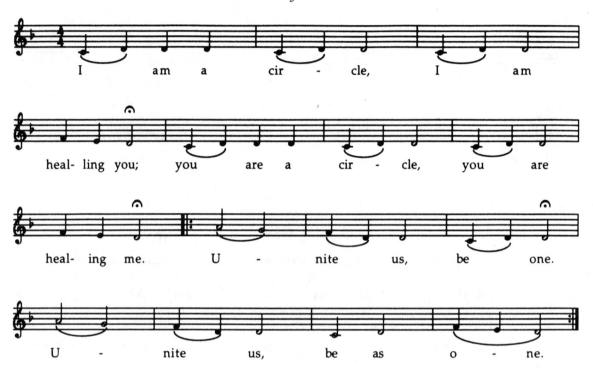

I am a cir - cle, I am

heal- ling you; you are a cir - cle, you are

heal- ing me. U - nite us, be one.

U - nite us, be as o - ne.

Sing slowly without accompaniment. This chant works well for building group trust, especially when intense healing work is being done. Stand and sway side by side in a large circle, your arms around your neighbor's shoulders. You can also chant and dance to heal your relationships.

**Dance:**
**With a partner:**
**1. I am a circle, I am healing you,**
Touch palms with your partner, creating a flowing circle of energy between you. Make eye contact as you send healing to your partner.
**2. You are a circle, you are healing me.**
Continue touching palms, creating a circuit of energy between you. Receive your partner's energy,
**3. Unite us be one.** One of you holds palms up, and the other palms down. Feel your oneness and connection.
4. **Unite us be as one.**
Connect more closely with your partner as it feels appropriate, hugging, etc.

# Tis a Gift to be Simple

*Traditional Shaker Song*

This chant connects us with our inner child, simplicity and innocence.

'Tis a gift to be sim- ple, 'tis a gift to be free. 'Tis a

gift to come down where you want to be. And

when you have come down to the place just right, you will

be in the val- ley of love and de- light. When the true sim-

pli - ci- ty is gained, to bow and to bend we shall

not be a- shamed. Turn, turn, 'twill be our de- light, 'til by

turn- ing, turn- ing we come round right.

# Healing By Night

*Native American Chant*
*Recorded by Prana* Second Chants, ©1983

By night I go on my way un- seen Then am I ho- ly then have I power to

heal men , then am I ho- ly then have I power to

heal men , then am I ho- ly then have I power to heal men à i o é i o

à i o é i o é i o

This women's healing chant can be adapted for anyone by changing the word 'men' to 'all'.

# Dark is the Path Alone

*Colin Ashleigh, Earth Spirit Community,* 1992

Round

2

Wheel turn-ing spin- ing, turn- ing, dark is the path a- lone

This healing chant helps us to confront the shadow aspects of our being, recognizing that we are part of the universal web, the wheel of life, ever changing and growing. As we embrace the dark within us, we can be reborn to the light. Use this chant to do the inner work associated with the coming of winter.

# I Will Not Be Afraid

*Rosie*

I will not be a- fraid to feel all my fears a- ny- more

I will not be a- fraid to feel all my fears a- ny more,

I will not be a- fraid I will not be a- fraid.

**Verses:**

I will not be afraid:

2. To say what I know anymore.
3. To dance all my dreams anymore.
4. To say what I love anymore.
5. To wonder and weep anymore.

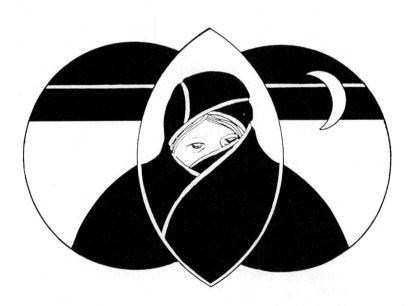

# All Beings Of the Earth

*Recorded on* All Beings of the Earth
*By EarthSpirit Community,* © 1985

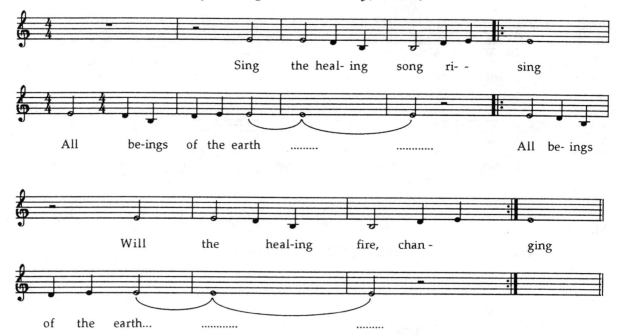

Sing    the heal- ing    song    ri - -    sing

All    be-ings    of the earth .........    ............    All    be- ings

Will    the    heal-ing    fire,    chan -    ging

of    the    earth...    ............    .........

This simple lyrical chant helps us enter into the depths of our being. Each line invokes healing by one of the elements—The air, fire, water, and earth. The EarthSpirit Community maintains this chant by a fire throughout a three day ritual every fall. It is also a powerful chant to use for planetary healing.

**Verses:**
Swim the healing deep, feeling.
Walk the healing Earth, being.

**Dance**: Divide into inner and outer circles:
*Outer circle* sings **All Beings of the Earth** as they side-step to the R in rhythm. Arms are stretched out to side at shoulder level, palms touching neighbor's palms.
*Inner circle* sings the verses with the following movements:
**Sing the healing song, rising**—Hold hands. Take six steps into the center of circle, raising arms slowly.
**Will the healing fire, changing**—Release hands. Clap your hands together four times on every other beat ( on 'will' 'heal' 'chang' and the silent beat ) as  you make a full turn clockwise in place accenting (stamping)  the same beat as the clap with your R foot.
**Swim the healing deep, feeling**—Take six steps back out  from the center, beginning with L foot. Arms cross each other two or three times in front of heart, undulating from the wrists like waves.
**Walk the healing Earth, being**—Make full turn counter-clockwise honoring the four directions, palms facing the earth, drawing in its magnetism.

# I Will be Gentle with Myself

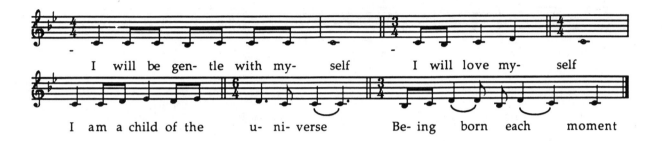

I will be gen- tle with my- self    I will love my- self

I am a child of the    u- ni- verse    Be- ing    born    each    moment

As you chant, allow an image to emerge of your inner child being acknowledged, supported, and loved. Ask the hurt child within you what healing she/he needs at this time.

**Verse:**
I will be gentle with myself.
I will heal myself.
I am a child of the universe,
held in love each moment.

Sing this chant to another person by substituting their name or the words 'you', 'yourself', 'he', 'she', etc. It also works well as a Blessingway Chant, to honor a woman before she gives birth.

## Giving Birth to Myself

I am a wo- man gi- ving birth to my- self
who is heal- ing my- self

Substitute 'I am a man', 'I am (name)' or use 'he' or 'she'.

## Give Me A Little Sunshine

*Jill Schumacher*

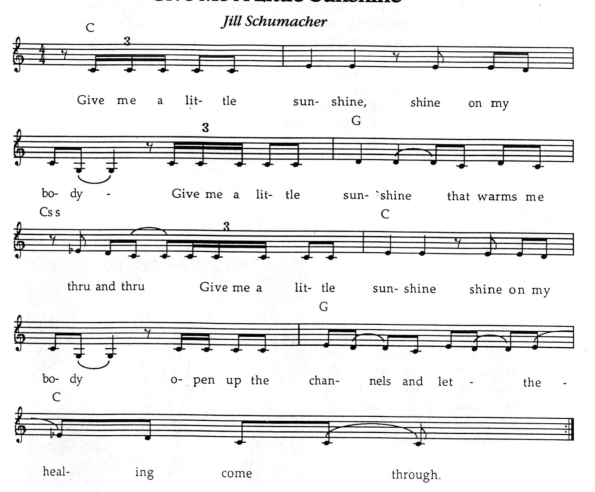

Give me a lit- tle sun- shine, shine on my
bo- dy - Give me a lit- tle sun- shine that warms me
thru and thru Give me a lit- tle sun- shine shine on my
bo- dy o- pen up the chan- nels and let - the -
heal- ing come through.

Chant as you stand in the sun, feeling its warmth and healing power.
Change the words 'let the healing' to 'let the spirit', 'let the power', etc.

## The Healing Power of Names

The following simple healing chants include ways to incorporate a person's name. When we are named, we recognize ourselves and are recognized and acknowledged by others. We reclaim our power and connect with a particular vibration / sound that expresses who we are. Many cultures have naming ceremonies where new names are taken at different stages of life as part of rites of passage.

### Naming Ceremony

*Take a moment to meditate on your name; see how you feel about it; what associations come up for you?*
*Chant your name over and over in a free form fashion. Try different nicknames you've had. What is the quality of energy, the vibrational tone? You may find a new name wants to be expressed, a name of power.*
*In a circle of others, chant your name as a way of introduction. Then let others reflect your vibration and essence as they sing your name back to you. They can create a sound tapestry, a sound portrait with your name/s as well as call out healing qualities, and empowering phrases. For example——Kate, is soft, open, powerful. Improvise freely, allowing images and sound to emerge which are unique for each person.*
*Finish your naming ceremony for each one by chanting `We welcome you '*

## You are Beautiful

| F | | C | C7 | F | | F7 | C7 |
|---|---|---|----|---|---|----|----|

( ) you are beaut- i- ful ( ) you are strong

| Bb | Am | Gm | C | F | C7 | F |
|----|----|----|---|---|----|---|

W on-der- ful to be with Carry us a-long ( ) Here's our lov-ing song.

## So Beautiful

( Ju- dy) so beau- ti- ful so, beau- ti -ful, is (Ju- dy)

**Verses:**
Healing..........so beautiful
Goddess.........
Love.............

## Oh, Celebrate

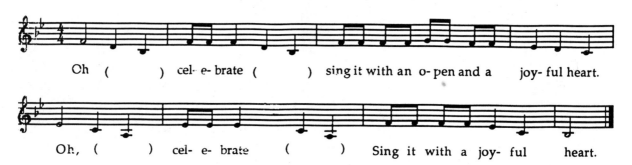

Oh ( ) cel- e- brate ( ) sing it with an o- pen and a joy- ful heart.

Oh, ( ) cel- e- brate ( ) Sing it with a joy- ful heart.

## We Love Your Love

(Hel - en) we love your love, we love your love, we love your love.

(Hel- en) we love your love, love your love to- day.

## All Shall Be Well

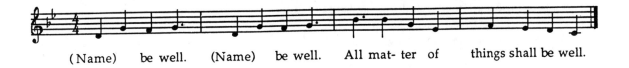

(Name) be well. (Name) be well. All mat- ter of things shall be well.

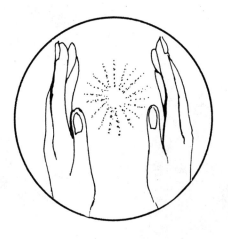

## The Power of Love

Love is the most powerful healing force of all. The following chants and dances invoke various aspects of love.

# Love is the Only Power

*Recorded by David Zeller on* Path of the Heart

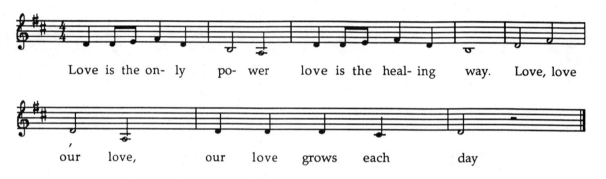

Love is the on- ly po- wer love is the heal- ing way. Love, love

our love, our love grows each day

**Dance:**
With partners:
**1. Love is the only power**
**2. Love is the healing way**
Face partner, looking into each other's eyes and beaming love out through heart, hands up, radiating energy.
**3. My love,**
Hands over your heart.
**4. Your love,**
Open out hands from the heart, feeling other's love.
**5. Our love grows each day**
Hold hands (or hug your partner) still beaming love to each other.

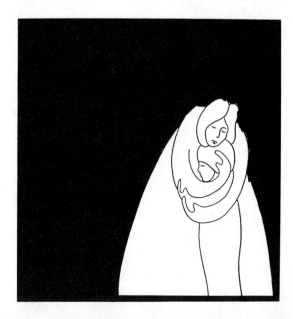

# Love, Love, Love

Round

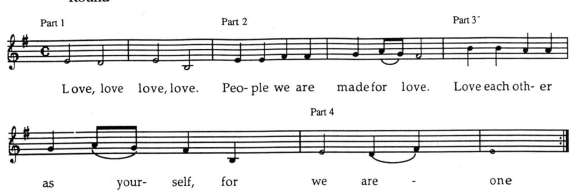

Love, love love, love. Peo- ple we are made for love. Love each oth- er

as your- self, for we are - one

A popular traditional chant, sung as a four part round. Many different verses have been written. See also *Lady Weave Your Circle* in Chapter Four and *Herne* in Chapter Five.

**Verses:**
Dear friends, dear friends (Substitute person's name)
Let me tell you how I feel.
You have given me such pleasure
I love you so.

Rose, Rose, Rose, Rose (use any person's name)
Let thy heart bloom as a flower
That I might offer you love's sweet fragrance
In this thy garden.

Love, Love, Love, Love
People this is your calling
Love your neighbor as yourself
For we are one. (God loves us all)

Peace, Peace, Peace, Peace
Crimes must end and wars must cease.
We shall learn to live together
Peace, peace, peace.

# O Dear Friend

Sing this as a counterpoint to *Love, Love, Love, Love.*

O dear friend take thy flight high in- to the spi- rit of

joy- ous light.

# Listen, Listen, Listen
*Paramahansa Yogananda*

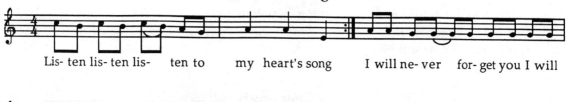

Lis- ten lis- ten lis- ten to my heart's song I will ne- ver for- get you I will

ne- ver fore- sake you

This chant is an old favorite which opens the heart.
**Verses:**
I will always remember. I will always be true
I will always love you  I will always serve you
**For women's's groups add:**
Listen Lady listen, to my heart's song.

# Start the Day with Love
*Words—Satya Sai Baba*

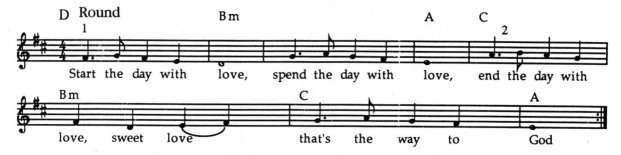

Start the day with love, spend the day with love, end the day with

love, sweet love that's the way to God

# I Surrender To Love

*Michael Stillwater*
*Recorded on* Heavensong Celebration Live,
© *Inner Harmony Music* 1984

Sing the men's and women's parts simultaneously

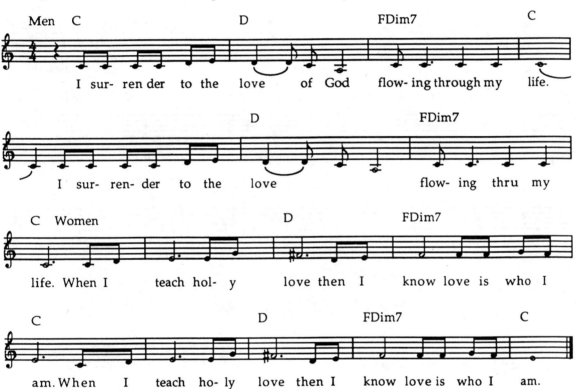

Men  C                    D          FDim7          C

I sur- ren der to the love of God flow- ing through my life.

D          FDim7

I sur- ren- der to the love flow- ing thru my

C  Women             D       FDim7

life. When I teach hol- y love then I know love is who I

C                       D     FDim7        C

am. When I teach ho- ly love then I know love is who I am.

# What Wondrous Love
*Traditional Quaker Song*

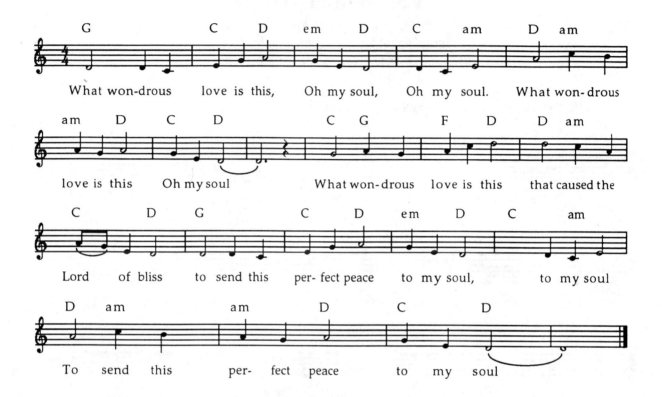

What won-drous love is this, Oh my soul, Oh my soul. What won-drous

love is this Oh my soul What won-drous love is this that caused the

Lord of bliss to send this per- fect peace to my soul, to my soul

To send this per- fect peace to my soul

# There's Only One Lover

There's on- ly one lo - - - ver. On- ly one lo - - -

ver. There's on- ly one lo - - - ver in the whole wide world.

There's only one mother/father/sister/brother 3x
There's only one lover in the whole wide world.
He is the Sun, the lover (She is the Moon, the lover)
and we are the rays of his (her)love.

There's only one lover, in the whole wide world
Ishk-Allah-Mahbud—lillah 3x
Mahbud li-lah
This Arabic phrase translates as, 'God is Love, Lover, and Beloved'.

Pronounciation: ish (like dish)—kah—la—ma—bood—lee—la

210

# Let My Heart Fly Open

*Jai Gopal*
*Recorded on* Swaha by *Amazing Grace* © 1974

Ah - - - - - I long for you, I long for you Ah

I live for you, and I die for you Ah - let me love you

Ah - Let my heart fly o- pen let me come to you. Let my heart fly op- en let me

come to you Ah - let me love you Ah - Let my heart fly o-pen let me

come to you. Let my heart fly o- pen let me come to you.

# Share Your Love

*Yaksan Valdez*

Sing in three parts.

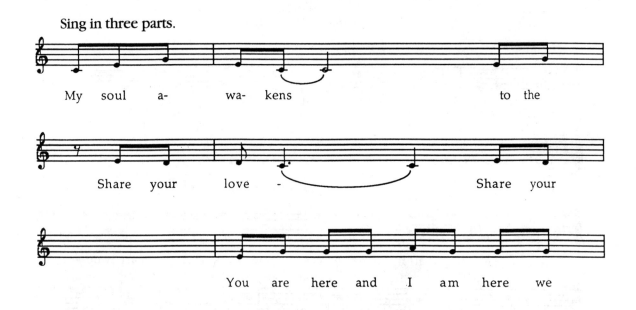

My soul a- wa- kens to the

Share your love - Share your

You are here and I am here we

light, and my spi- rit re- joi- ces in the

love - with the

share the world to-ge- ther. You are here and I am here we

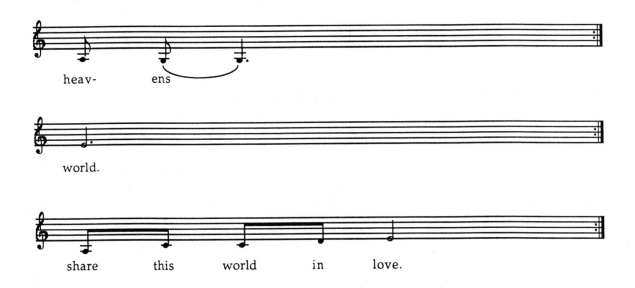

heav- ens

world.

share this world in love.

An important aspect of expressing and sharing our love is through giving and receiving.

# From You I Receive

*Nathan L. Segal © 1968*
*Recorded on* Joseph and Nathan

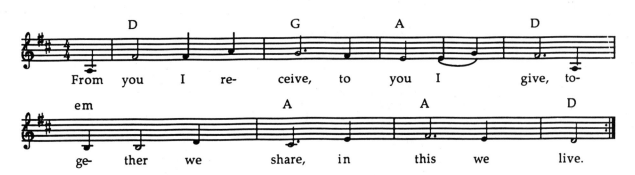

From you I re- ceive, to you I give, to-

ge- ther we share, in this we live.

# Our Magic is Our Giveaway

*Skip Shukmam*

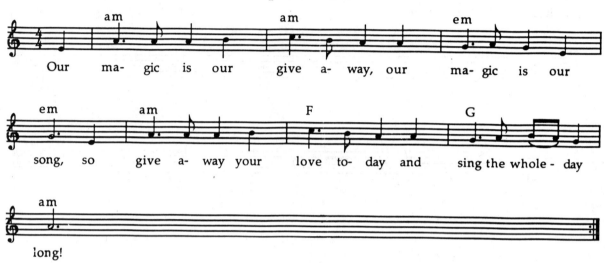

Our ma- gic is our give a- way, our ma- gic is our

song, so give a- way your love to- day and sing the whole - day

long!

Sing these chants as part of a Give-away ceremony traditionally done in Native American tribes. It can be adapted for any group. The 'giveaway' is a Plains Indian term used by such tribes as the Blackfoot and Cheyenne. It means to give selflessly without expectation of return. As we give in this way, we receive back tenfold. When others give to us, we 'give away' offerings to them. In Native American traditions, for example, cornmeal or tobacco is 'given away' to the earth in thankfulness for all she has given.

## Give-away Ceremony

To be done with at least six people. All participants bring a gift to share that is special to them. It can represent something you are ready to let go of in your life.

*Put the gifts on a blanket, wrapped or not. With smaller groups each person talks about the significance of their gift as everyone listens. With larger groups, gifts are left anonymously.*

*Everyone sits in a circle and in a ceremonial way (perhaps going from the oldest to the youngest, or beginning in one of the directions and going around), each person goes one at a time to the blanket and selects a gift.*

*At the end, the givers and receivers may want to come together and share with each other.*

# Chapter Seven

# Peace and Unity

# Peace and Unity

## Meditation—Peace and Unity

*Go to a beautiful, peaceful place in nature.
Tune into the rhythm of your breath. As you exhale, let go
of any preoccupations and anxieties. Allow your mind to
become quiet; experience a deep sense of peace and oneness
with all. Feel your thoughts of peace and unity touch and
transform all the places on the planet that are full of pain,
suffering, violence and turmoil. As you chant the mantra
AUM, let your prayers spiral outward toward your loved
ones and into the world. Send healing vibrations to all
beings.*

## Connecting with the Sacred Self

The following chants and dances help us connect with our sacred self and experience inner peace and oneness.

# All Knowing Spirit Within Me

*Michael Tierra*

Three part round

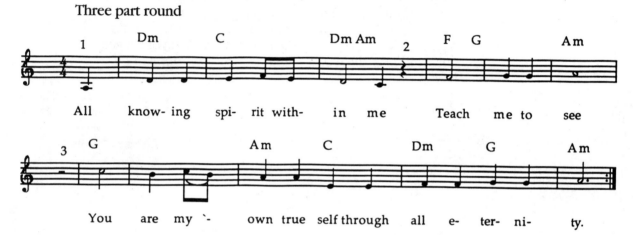

All know-ing spi- rit with- in me Teach me to see You are my own true self through all e- ter- ni- ty.

# The Circle Shapes Us

*Deirdre Pulgram Arthen, EarthSpirit Community*
*Recorded on* All Beings of the Earth © 1984

The cir- cle shapes us bo-dy and mind Heart and soul are one.

# Holy Spirit Within

*Mark Anderson*

Ho- ly    spir- it    with    in me        Help me to move    in- to

I ask for    beaut- ty in my   self - -        I ask    for beau- ty in the

that    which I am        Help me to love    the    whole    of the

world - -        I ask    for beau- ty for        all - of my

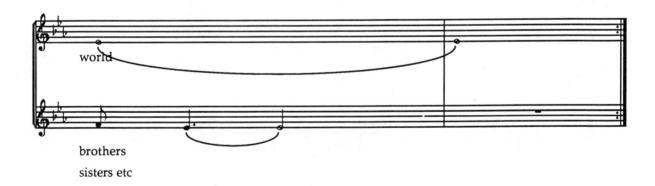

world

brothers
sisters etc

Sing in two parts, with two circles facing each other. The women and men each sing a part and then switch. Add simple movements for each part.

# I Am As God Created Me

*Michael Stillwater*
*Recorded on* You Belong To Love, *Inner Harmony Music* © 1988

Sing in four parts:

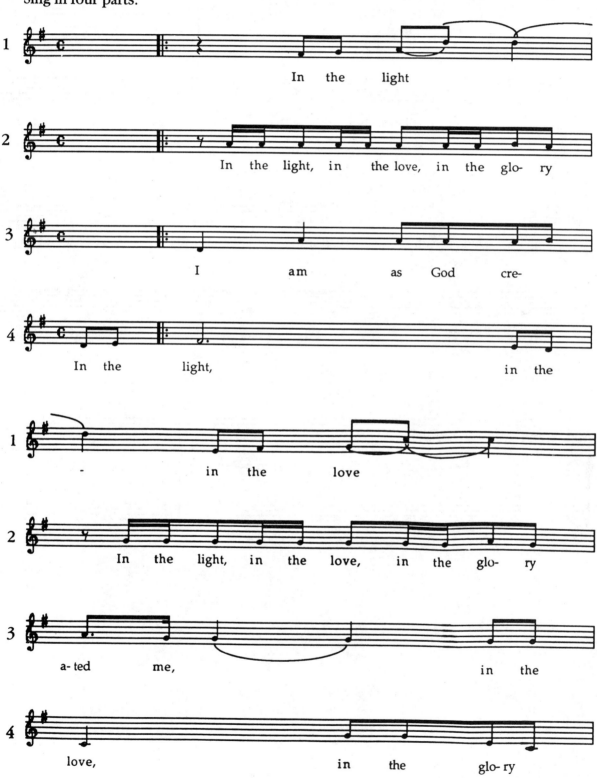

1  In the glo- ry of God I am.

2  In the light, in the love, in the glo - ry I am.

3  light, in the love, in the glo - ry

4  of God I am. In the

## Yes, God is Real

Yes, God is real, real in my Soul Yes, God is real, for he has

washed and made me whole - His love for me shines like pure gold,

yes, God is real for I can feel God in my Soul.

# I Am

*David Casselman* © 1982

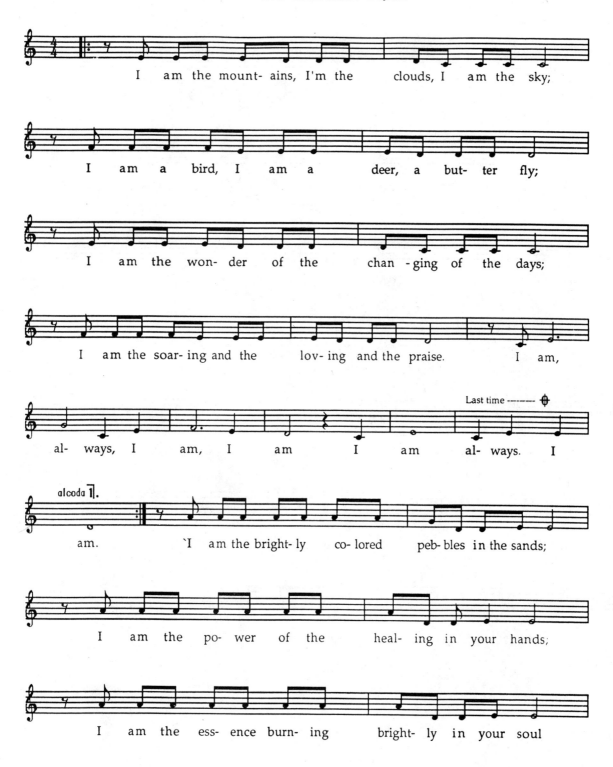

I am the mount- ains, I'm the clouds, I am the sky;

I am a bird, I am a deer, a but- ter fly;

I am the won- der of the chan -ging of the days;

I am the soar- ing and the lov- ing and the praise. I am,

Last time

al- ways, I am, I am I am al- ways. I

alcoda 1.

am. `I am the bright- ly co- lored peb- bles in the sands;

I am the po- wer of the heal- ing in your hands;

I am the ess- ence burn- ing bright- ly in your soul

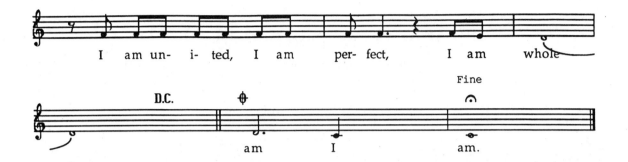

I am un- i- ted, I am per- fect, I am whole

am I am.

**Verses:**
I am singing, I am dancing, I am free.
I am the dust, and now a seed, and now a tree.
I am the message that is heard by everyone.
I am the freedom, and the glory and the sun.
**Chorus**–I am, always etc. Then sing second part
I am the blending of the people everywhere
I am awake, I am alive, I am aware.
I am the miracle of living everyday
I am the universe, and this is what I say,
**Chorus**

# Ya No Ah

*Wabun–Bear Tribe*
*Recorded on* The Dawning–Chants of the Medicine Wheel

Ya no ah no ah né    Ya no ah no ah né    Ya no ah no ah né

ya    no    ah    no    ah    né    ya

This Native American Chant helps us quiet the chatter of our minds and find a calm clear space within. Chant the phrase over and over; a second voice comes in after the first two measures. Experiment with making the sounds more nasal, especially the N sounds. Feel them resonate deep into your skull, stimulating all the cells in your brain. Feel the vibration of the Ah/Ya sounds opening your heart.

**Dance:**
Link arms and do the side–step, Grandmother or Ghost dance steps in a circle, facing in. As you close your eyes and nasalize your sound, you will experience an altered state quickly. If possible, do the chant/dance continuously for an hour or longer. Make sure to ground yourself well when you are done.

# My Words Are Tied in One
*Yokuts Indian Prayer*

My words are tied in one with the great mount- ain

with the great rocks with the great trees. In one with my

bo- dy and my heart

Will you all help me with su- per- na- tu- ral pow- er. And

you day and you night, all of you see me one with this

earth.

# Return Again

*Words: Ronnie Kahn  Music. Shlomo Carlebach*

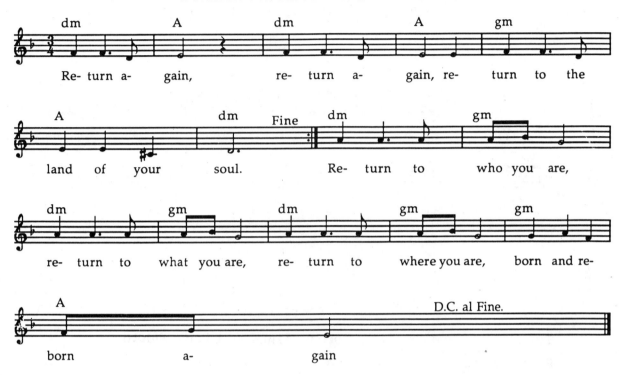

This song from the Jewish tradition connects us with the essence of our being, and unites us with our soul. It invokes a process of inner rebirth. You can also sing it with the syllable Li Li Li (like die) as a nigun, wordless chant.

**Dance:**

**1. Return again, return again**
Take one step in, raising arms, then one step back, lowering arms.

**2. Return to the home of your (my) soul**
Separate and spin alone, feeling your connection with your soul.

**3. Repeat #1**

**4. Repeat #2**—This time all move into the center of the circle, raising arms upward, uniting with the universal source.

**5. Return to who you are (who I am)**
   **Return to what you are (what I am)**
   **Return to where you are born (where I am born)**
Drop hands, extend arms out and spin alone slowly out from center, in same direction throughout. Feel yourself unite with your soul, your source and rebirth.

**6. And re—born again**
On the last turn (at periphery of circle) bring hands down slowly and cross them over your heart.

# Thula Kleziyo (Thula Nhliziyo)

*Zulu Chant from South Africa*
*Joseph and Nellie Shabalaya, 1988*

Thu la kle zi    o na    la pa se ka ya    Eh ka ya na

la        pa        se        ka        ya

**Translation:** ' Be still my heart, wherever I am, I am at home with you.'

**Pronounciation:**    Too la klay zee yo

Nala pa se ka (like eye) ya

Eh ka ya

Na la pa se ka ya

**Dance**: (Traditional )
Move around a circle one behind the other, in a
counterclockwise direction.
**Thul - a -kle- zi - yo na la pa se ka ya 2x** On the
accented beats, make small jump/lunge forward and
down onto R foot, bending R knee. Bend torso/head
down and forward. On the beats in between, shift
weight to L foot, straighten both knees, arch torso/head
up and back. On the accented beats, cross your hands
over your heart. On other beats, bring hands off heart,
about a foot in front of your chest, still crossed. Repeat
twice.
**E ka ya na la pa se ka ya 2x** Arch torso/ head
back, arms out to side at shoulder level, hands with
palms facing out, fingers seperated like a fan, pointing
skyward. Walk forward with syncopated rhythm—
swaying body and hands side to side. Repeat twice.
Then begin again.

# Inner Peace and Harmony

The following chants help us to unify all aspects of our being; to balance the masculine and feminine polarities within us. (Before doing the following meditation, explore the feminine and masculine separately in Chapter's Four and Five.)

## Meditation—Balancing the Masculine and Feminine

*Allow an image to emerge of the feminine aspect of your being. Begin to embody and express this feminine energy, allowing sound and movement to come forth. Experiment with using predominantly the left side of your body. Then, when you feel ready, allow an image of your masculine aspect to emerge. Begin to embody and express this masculine energy, creating a dance and song, experimenting with your right side. Move and use vocal sounds freely; shift back and forth between the two sides, exploring both polarities fully. Begin a dialogue between your feminine and masculine aspects, between your left and right sides. How do they interact? What do they say to each other? What do they need from each other for their mutual healing?*

*Gradually notice the boundaries between them merge and change. Allow your movements to blend and transform into a new dance, which integrates the two sides. Let a symbol emerge which represents the union of your feminine and masculine polarities. It may not come immediately, but know that the process has begun and is working within you. Continue your dance until you feel complete, then open your eyes slowly.*

*End with a simple ritual: Honor your feminine by drinking blessed water out of a chalice with your left hand. Celebrate your masculine by fanning the fire from a candle flame into your heart with your right hand. Feel the two energies merge within your being.*

227

# There's a Man/Woman in You

This chant honors the unification and harmony of all aspects of our being, the many voices within us—the God/Goddess, the inner man, woman and child. By acknowledging all these parts, we heal ourselves and come into wholeness.

There's a    man in me. There's a    man in you. There's a    wo-man in    me. There's a

wo-man in    you. There's a    child    in    me, there's a    child in you. There's a

God    in    me,    there's    a    God    in    you.

**Verse:**
And the man in me loves the man in you.
And the woman in me loves the woman in you.
And the child in me loves the child in you.
And the God in me, is the God in you.

# I am One With the Heart of the Mother/Father

*Michael Stillwater*
*Recorded on* Voices of the Heart, *Inner Harmony Music* © 1987

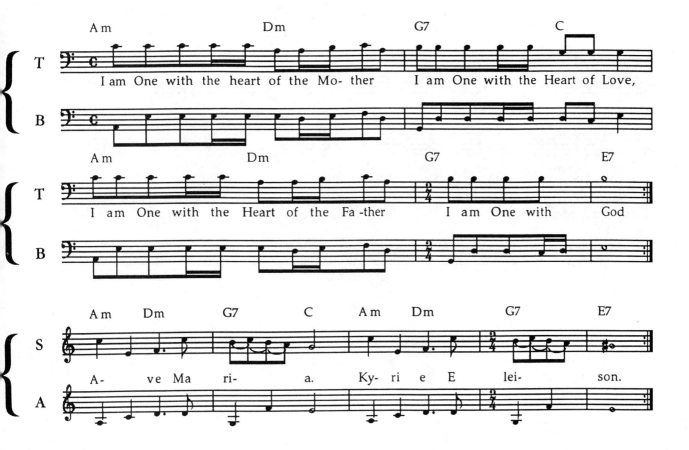

Ave Maria means Hail Mary, expression of the Divine Feminine. Kyrie Eleison means 'Lord have mercy' or 'God is mercy'.

# You Are My Mother/Father

*Fantuzzi*

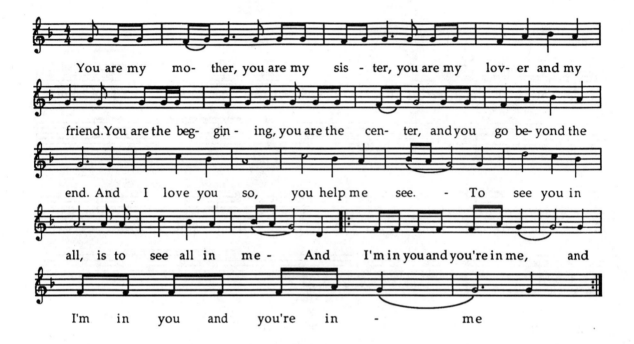

You are my mo- ther, you are my sis - ter, you are my lov- er and my

friend. You are the beg- gin - ing, you are the cen- ter, and you go be- yond the

end. And I love you so, you help me see. - To see you in

all, is to see all in me - And I'm in you and you're in me, and

I'm in you and you're in - me

**Verses:**

You are my father, you are my brother,
you are my lover, you are my friend.

You are the mountains, you are the ocean,
you are the sky, you are my friend.

You are the Buddha, you are the Krishna,
You are the Christ, you are my friend.

# Celebration and Joy

These chants and dances celebrate the joy of being and working together and our power to create a peaceful planet.

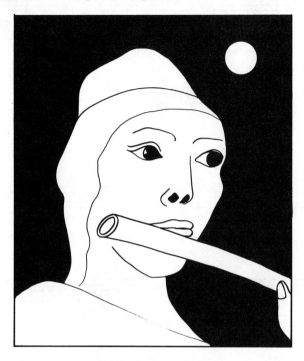

## Asite Dumayla
*African Chant*

A- si- te    Du- may- la        A- bu te

Du- may- la        As- i- te

Translation: 'Hello brothers and sisters. Let us celebrate together.'

**Dance:**

Make two rows, or an inner and outer circle with dancers facing each other maintaining eye contact. On the word Dumayla, take a step each time: first one step to *side* (R foot to side and L foot meets the R) then one step *forward* in greeting, then one step *back*. Then start the pattern again to the side, advancing each time to greet new partner. Feel the syncopation and add a slight bounce to your step. Hold hands—raise them up to W as you step forward; lower them to V as you step back; hold them down in V as you side–step.

231

# Bon Ca Va a de Kele

*W. African Chant from the borders of Togo and Ghana*
*Recorded by Prana on* Seven Seasons Suns, *1987*

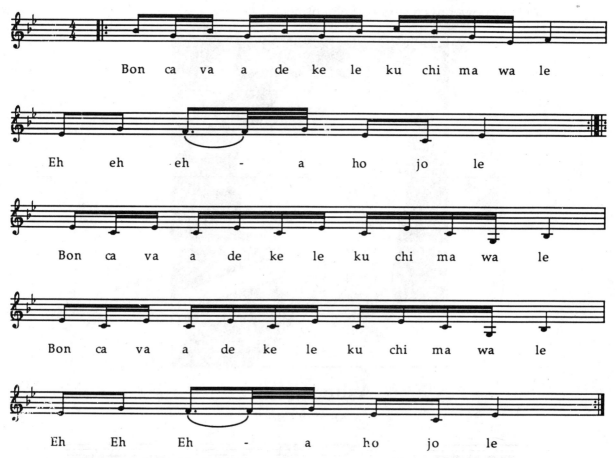

Bon ca va a de ke le ku chi ma wa le

Eh eh eh - a ho jo le

Bon ca va a de ke le ku chi ma wa le

Bon ca va a de ke le ku chi ma wa le

Eh Eh Eh - a ho jo le

The words translate as: 'Hello. How are you? Now we are together, let us play.'

232

# Hida

This Hebrew chant is sung as a beautiful two part round. Hi - da is a nigun (nonsense syllable) which evokes the quality of joy and devotion. Don't forget to put the clap in where noted.

# Sing Together

# Let's Be Beginning

233

# Nigun

*Shlomo Carlebach*

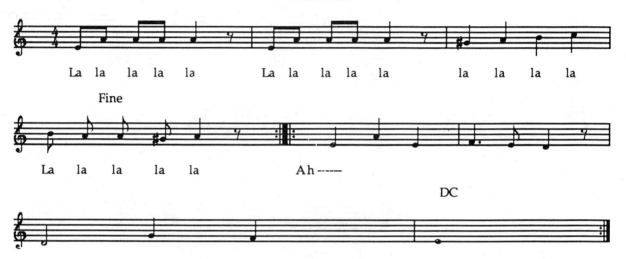

La la  la  la  la        La  la  la  la  la        la  la  la  la

Fine

La  la  la  la  la        Ah ------

DC

Niguns, from the Jewish tradition, are sung without words allowing you to go deep into the spirit of the music.

**Dance:**
Do a simple circle or snake dance. Begin slowly. Gradually get faster and then slow down again.

# Praise Ye the Lord With Joy

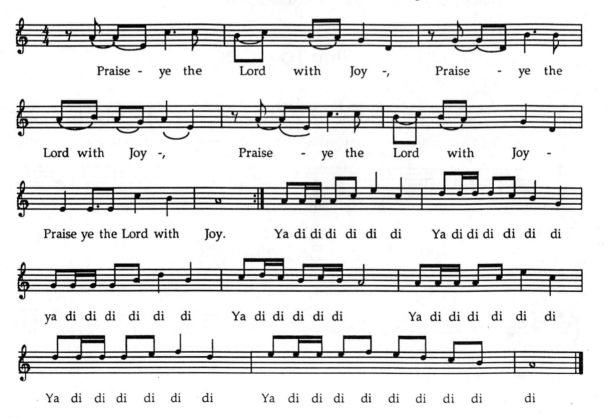

Praise - ye the   Lord   with   Joy -,   Praise   - ye the

Lord with   Joy -,        Praise   - ye the   Lord   with   Joy -

Praise ye the Lord with   Joy.   Ya di di di di di di di   Ya di di di di di di di

ya di di di di di di di   Ya di di di di di di   Ya di di di di di di di

Ya di di di di di di di   Ya di di di di di di di di di   di

# Rock 'a My Soul

This chant is good for children. Accompany it with a simple, joyful childlike dance.

# Sing And Rejoice

*W.H. Bradbury*

Round

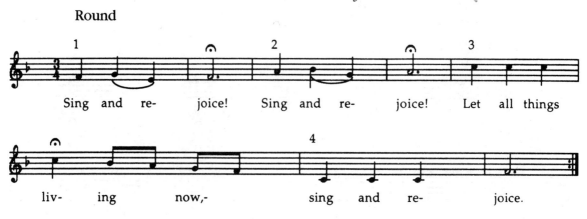

Sing and re-joice! Sing and re-joice! Let all things

liv-ing now,- sing and re-joice.

**Verses:**
Hosanna, Hosanana
And on Earth peace to all
Folk of good will.

# Won' t You Rock Us

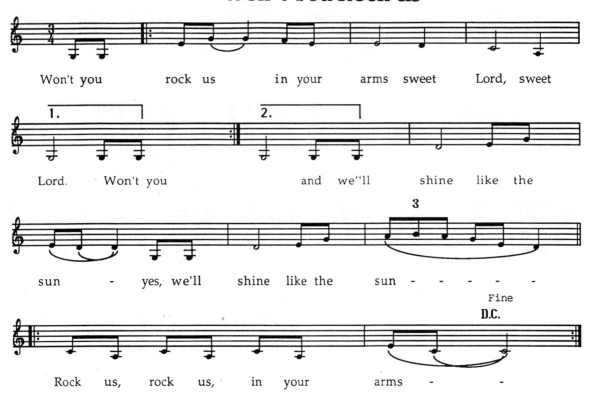

Won't you rock us in your arms sweet Lord, sweet

Lord. Won't you and we''ll shine like the

sun - yes, we'll shine like the sun - - - - -

Fine

D.C.

Rock us, rock us, in your arms - -

# Rejoice in the Lord

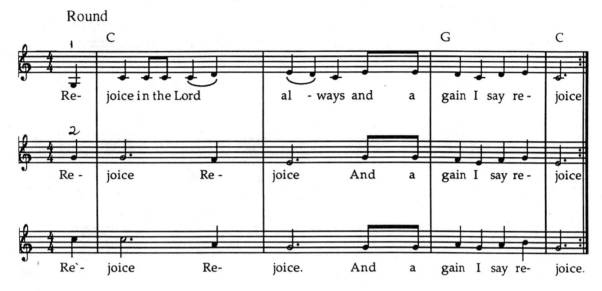

# Alleluya/Glory

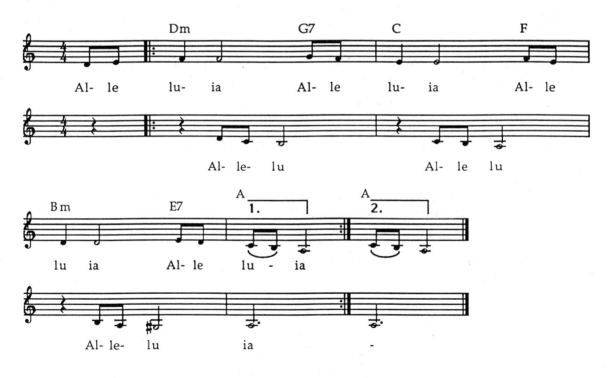

**Verse:**
Glory Glory

# If the People Lived Their Lives

*Traditional Russian Folk Song*

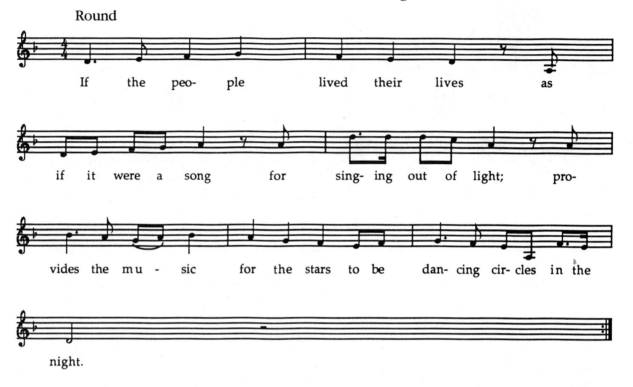

Round

If the peo- ple lived their lives as if it were a song for sing- ing out of light; pro- vides the mu - sic for the stars to be dan- cing cir- cles in the night.

Substitute other words such as 'If the women lived their lives'

**Dance:**

**If the people lived their lives**
All move around in a circle, holding hands.

**As if it were a song**
Move into the center raising hands above head.

**For singing out of light**
Release hands and individually spin out from center, returning to the original circle. Raise arms towards heavens, invoking light.

**Provides the music for the stars**
Standing in place, sway from side to side, arms raised toward stars.

**To be dancing circles in the night.**
Spin in place, arms still raised toward stars.
Repeat.

# We Are One in the Spirit

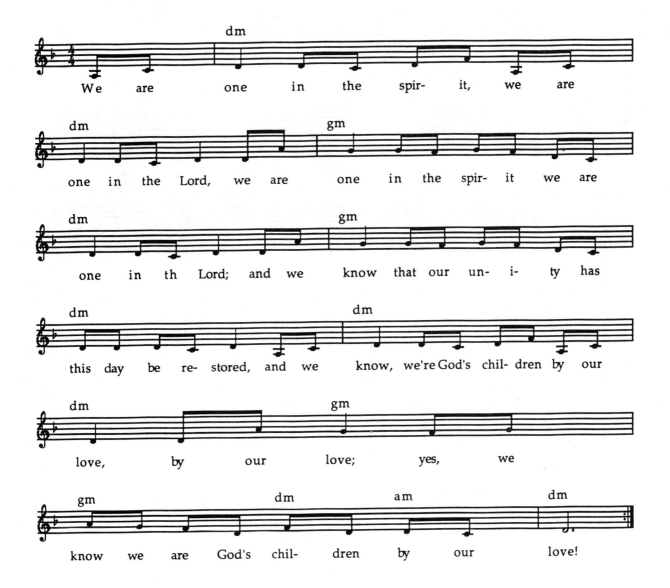

**Verses:**

We will walk with each other, we will walk hand in hand.
And together we'll spread the word that God is in our land.

We will work with each other, we will work side by side
And we're finding our dignity by knowing God inside.

**Other verse possibility:** (By Kate Marks)

We are one with the spirit, we are one with the earth

And we know that our unity will bring forth new birth

And we know we're Gaia's children by our love by our love, yes

we know we're Gaia's children by our love.

# Under the Sky

Round               2

Un- der the sky, un- der the sky, we are all

one fa- mi- ly, un- der the sky, we are all one

fa- mi- ly un- der the sky!

# Wehnahani Yo

*Hopi Friendship Song*

Weh na ha ni yo - ey ya ey ya yeh ey ya

D.C.

ey ey ey ey ya (3 times) wey na ha ni ey ey ey ey ya

**Dance:**
Form a circle or two lines facing each other. Take four steps to the right, then four steps to the left. Swing arms alternately.

## Peace on Earth

The following chants are good to use for peace meditations and seasonal ceremonies. As you chant, unite your heart and voice with others. Send your peaceful thoughts, healing energy, prayers and blessings out into the world.

# Light a Candle For Peace

*Recorded on* Heartsongs *by Lia Argo*

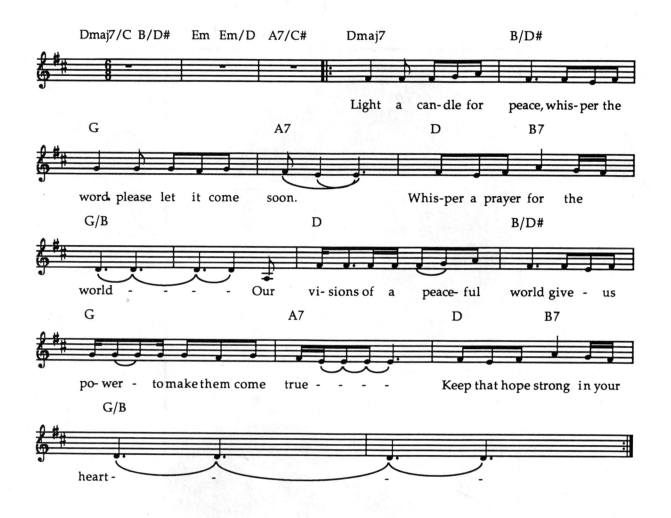

# Om Shanti

*Hindu Peace Chant*

# I Love the People

I love the peo- ple and I love the sea- sons

**Verses**

I love the rivers that flow to the ocean.
The people united will not be defeated.
Come out of your houses and take a stand!
Stand for the future, stand for the children;
Struggle in courage, struggle in peace.

# Vine and Fig Tree

*From Hebrew Bible—Isaiah 2:4 Micah 4:3*
*English translation: Leah M. Jaffe and Fran Minkoff*

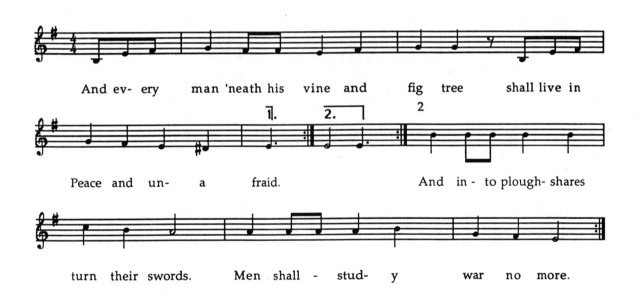

And ev- ery man 'neath his vine and fig tree shall live in

Peace and un- a fraid. And in - to plough- shares

turn their swords. Men shall - stud- y war no more.

**Verse:** In Hebrew
Lo yisa goy el goy cherev
Lo yilmedu od milchama (repeat)
Lo yisa goy el goy cherev
Lo yilmedu od milchama (repeat)

# Peace on Earth

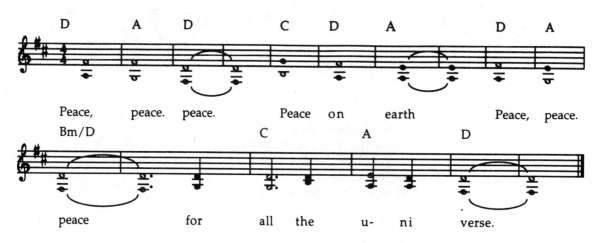

Peace,     peace.    peace.     Peace    on     earth     Peace,   peace.

peace         for     all    the    u-    ni     verse.

# May All Beings Be Well

*Words: Traditional    Music: Joe and Guin Miller*

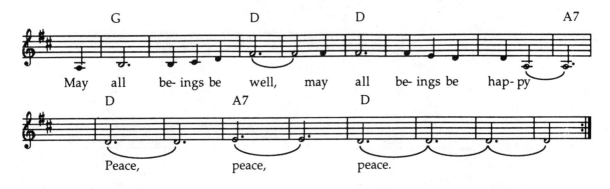

May    all    be- ings be    well,    may    all    be- ings be    hap- py

Peace,        peace,         peace.

# Sanctify the Earth

*David Casselman*
*Recorded on* Sanctify the Earth © 1981

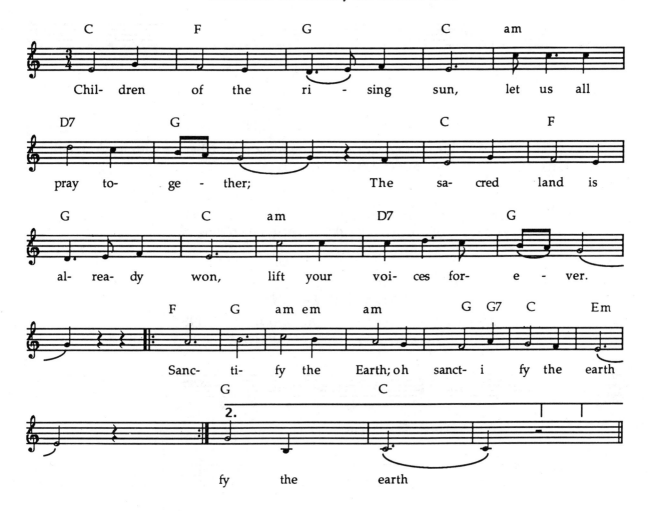

Verse:
Children of the rolling hills,
Let us all pray together.
Free hand, free hearts, free souls, free wills,
Lift your voices forever.
**Chorus**
Children of the sacred lake,
Let us all pray together.
Your tears may fall and breath may quake
Lift your voices forever.
**Chorus**
Children of the stormy seas,
Let us all pray together.
The power of love will set us free
Lift your voices forever.

# Ele Ele Tau Mai

*Hawaiian Peace Chant*

E-    le    e-    le         ta-    u    mai

It means 'May great peace descend' Pronounce it Eli (rhymes with Jelly) Tau (rhymes with How) Mai (rhymes with My).

**Dance:**
Start with your arms above your head. Draw them slowly toward the earth, palms facing down. Focus on creating peace and harmony on the planet.

# Peace Be To You

*Michael Stillwater © Inner Harmony Music, 1987*
*Recorded on* Voices of the Heart

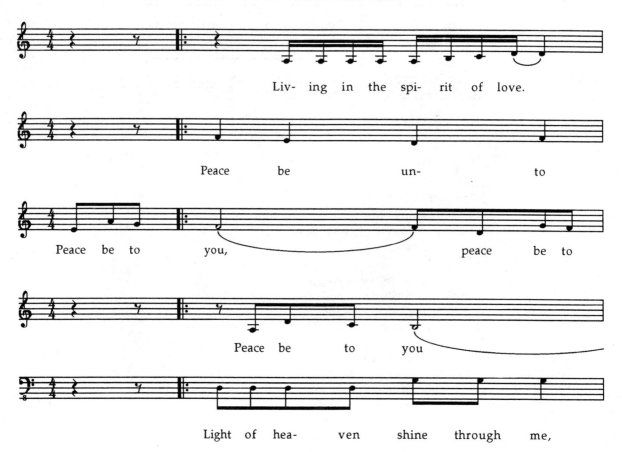

Liv- ing in the spi- rit of love.

Peace    be    un-    to

Peace  be  to    you,                peace  be  to

Peace  be    to    you

Light  of  hea- ven    shine    through    me,

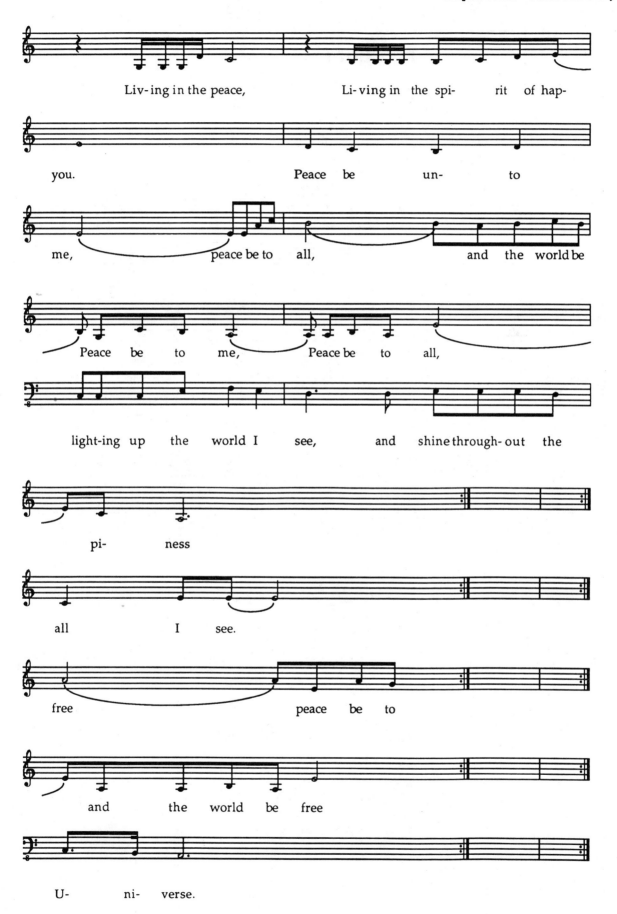

Liv-ing in the peace,  Li-ving in the spi-  rit of hap-

you.  Peace  be  un-  to

me,  peace be to  all,  and  the world be

Peace  be  to  me,  Peace be  to  all,

light-ing up  the  world I  see,  and  shine through-out  the

pi-  ness

all  I  see.

free  peace  be  to

and  the  world  be  free

U-  ni-  verse.

# Freedom is Coming

*South Africa.*
*Recorded on* Spread Your Rainbow Wings

Sing in two parts. Add other words such as 'Peace is coming'.

yes I know Oh yes I know, Free- dom is

com- ing Free- dom is com- ing Free- dom is

com- ing Oh yes I know Oh yes I know Oh yes I know Oh

com- ing Oh yes I know Oh free-dom is com- ing, Free-dom is

yes I know Free- dom is com- ing Oh yes I know.

com- ing Oh, free- dom is com- ing, Oh yes I know.

## Shabbat Shalom

'Peace on this sabbath day.' Shabbat is the Sabbath, the seventh day of the week set aside by Jews for rest and worship (from sunset Friday to sunset Saturday.)

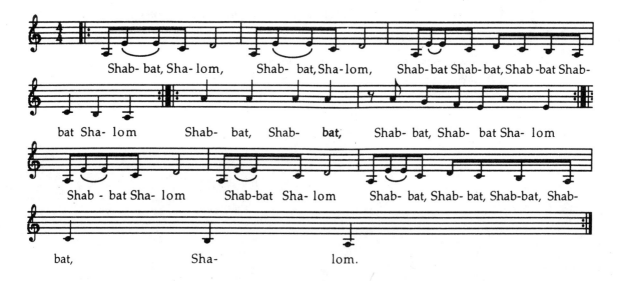

Shab- bat, Sha- lom, Shab- bat, Sha- lom, Shab- bat Shab- bat, Shab -bat Shab-

bat Sha- lom Shab- bat, Shab- **bat,** Shab- bat, Shab- bat Sha- lom

Shab - bat Sha- lom Shab-bat Sha- lom Shab- bat, Shab- bat, Shab-bat, Shab-

bat, Sha- lom.

# Havenu Shalom

*Hebrew Peace Chant*

Ha- ve nu    sha- lom A-    le- chem    Ha- ve -nu

sha- lom A-    le- chem    Ha- ve- nu    Sha - lom A-

le- chem,    Ha- ve- nu    Sha- lom, Sha- lom    Sha-lom A-    le chem.

**Dance:**
**Line 1 and 2**
Do the side—step (or the grapevine step) around the circle,
holding hands.
**Line 3**
Move into the center, raising arms up.
**Line 4**
Let go of your hands. Open arms. Spin out individually from the
center back to the original circle.
**Repeat**
**With partners:**
On first three lines move around to three different people and bless
each one. Then, on final line, spin alone ending up with new
partner.
**Verse written for the Goddess to the same melody. Words by
Steve Posch**
Oh, may the Goddess be with me/you—3x
Goddess, Goddess, Goddess be with me/you
Oh may the Goddess protect me/you—3x
Goddess, Goddess, Goddess protect me/you.

# Dona Nobis Pacem

*W. A. Mozart (1756–91)*

Round and 3 part canon. This translates as 'Give Us Peace'.

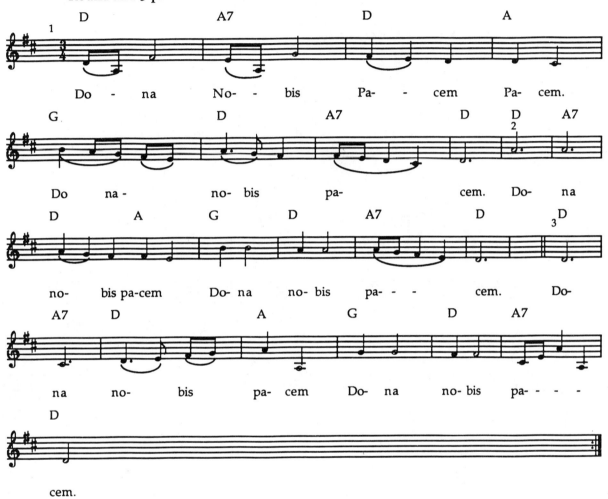

# Da Pacem

Round

These two chants, sung in Latin, celebrate Peace.

## Gratitude and Blessings

### Meditation—Giving Thanks

*Close your eyes. Take some time to review your life.*
*Get in touch with the things for which you are grateful.*
*Honor and acknowledge the abundance and blessings you*
*have received. In a circle, let each person say 'I am thankful*
*for _____'.*

# Thank You for This Day
*Native American Church*

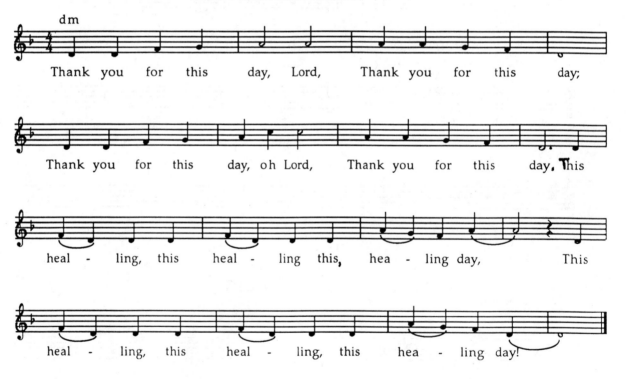

Thank you for this day, Lord, Thank you for this day;

Thank you for this day, oh Lord, Thank you for this day. This

heal - ling, this heal - ling this, hea - ling day, This

heal - ling, this heal - ling, this hea - ling day!

**Verses:**
Add your own lines such as: 'Thank you for this Life, this food,
these friends, etc.' Sing it around a circle with each person
adding a line.

# Thank You Mother Earth

*Susan Arrow* © 1985
*Recorded on* Welcome Sweet Pleasure

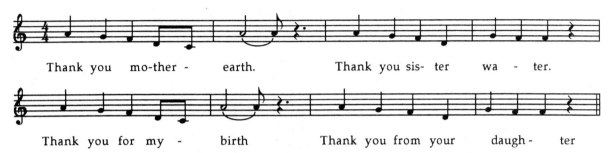

Thank you   mo-ther -   earth.     Thank you sis- ter    wa - ter.

Thank you for my -    birth     Thank you from your    daugh - ter

A grace to sing over food or at other times of gratitude. It is also good to use to dismiss the four elements at the end of a ritual.

**Verse:**
Thank you Brother Sun
Thank you Air in motion
Thank you Everyone
Earth, Air, Sun and Ocean.

# Let us Give Thanks

*Michael Tierra*

Round

Let us gi -ve thanks for -   this new day.   May we all - walk - in a

sac-        red        way.

# For Food and Joy

Greek Round

Ya tow fa-ee    Ya tee hara    S'- ef- ha- ri- sto    The- e.
For this food,    and our joy,    Giv- er of all, we    thank Thee

# Thank You For the World

Thank you for the world so sweet; thank you for the food we eat;

thank you for the birds that sing; thank you God for ev' ry- thing.

# Tallis Canon

*Words: Thomas Ken, 1695 Music: Thomas Tallis, 1565*

Succeeding voices enter after 'All praise to Thee'

All praise to thee, my God, this night, for all of the bless-ings

of the light; keep me, o keep me, king of kings be-

neath Thine own al- might- y wings.

# O Thou Sustainer

*Words: Hazrat Inayat Khan*

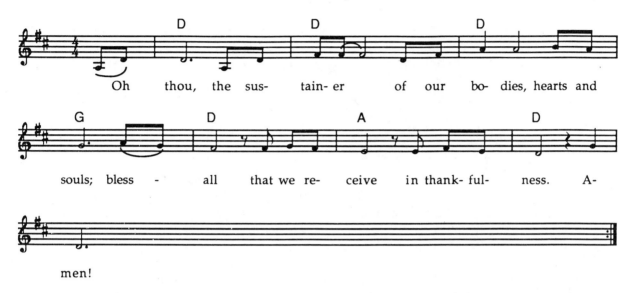

Oh thou, the sus- tain- er of our bo- dies, hearts and souls; bless - all that we re- ceive in thank- ful- ness. A- men!

Sing this as a grace and blessings before meals. It comes to us from the Sufi community, the Sufi Order of the West.

# Praise Unto the God and Goddess

Round

Praise un- to the God and God dess for all of the bless- ings that they bring

# For Health and Strength

Round

For health and strength and dai- ly food we praise Thy name, O God

# Coming Full Circle

These final closing chants help us to say goodbye, mark an ending, close a meeting or ceremony. They give us perspective on our lives and help us to remember that we have no beginning or ending but are part of the universal circle, the cycle of birth and death.

### Meditation—Endings

*Go back through your life and recall memories and experiences that involved endings, times when something came to completion. These could be events such as a divorce, a death, a graduation or a move to a new home or job. How have you marked and honored the transitions and endings in your life? How have these endings and 'deaths' been initiations, catalysts for change and transformation?*

*Write down on pieces of paper what it is that you need to let go of in your life at this time in order to begin a new cycle. When you are ready, take the pieces of paper and burn them as you voice out loud what you are releasing and what you are calling forth as you move into the new.*

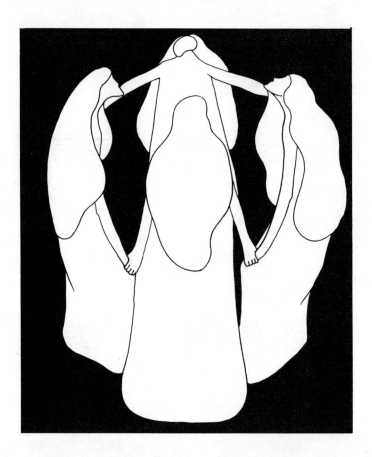

# We Are a Circle Within a Circle

*Rick Hamouris © Forever Forests, 1986*
*Recorded on* Welcome to Annwfn

We are a cir- cle wi- thin a cir- cle with no be-

You hear us sing; you hear us sigh. Now hear us

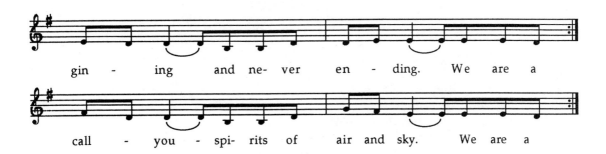

gin - ing and ne- ver en- ding. We are a

call - you - spi- rits of air and sky. We are a

**Verses:**

The chorus is sung twice at the beginning, at the end and after each verse. It is also very catchy sung alone. The same tune is used for all verses except #4.

Inside our hearts there lies a spark
Love and desire, a burning fire.

Within our blood, within our tears
There lies the altar of living water.

Take our fear, take our pain
Take the darkness into the earth again.

The circle closes between the worlds
To mark the sacred space, where we come face to face.

**Dance:**

A simple dance can accompany the chorus part. Make several circles within circles as you weave a spiral or chain dance. Look deeply into the eyes of others as you pass by them.

# No End to the Circle

*Starhawk*© 1981
*Recorded on* Let it Begin Now, *Reclaiming Collective,* 1992

There is no end to the cir- cle, no end; there is no end to

life there is no end

**Verses:** (For the Goddess Invocation)
1. For you can see me in your eyes
When they are mirrored by a friend
**Refrain**
For I am the power to begin
I dream and bring to birth what's never been
There is no end to freedom, no end
There is no end to life, there is no end
**Refrain**
2. And you can hear me in your voice
And feel me in each breath that you breathe in
**Refrain**
I am the power to sustain
I am the ripened fruit and growing grain
There is no end to my abundance, no end
There is no end to life, there is no end
**Refrain**
3. And you can feel me in your heart
When it beats with the heart of a friend
**Refrain**
And I am the power to end
I am the Crone who cuts the cord I spin
Though all things that are born must die again
There is no end to life there is no end
**Refrain**
4. For all proceeds from me and all returns
All that returns to me comes forth again
**Refrain**
I am the honey taste of passion's heat
The fear running through your heartbeat
I am dancing through your lightened feet
Desire so fierce and love so sweet.
**Refrain**

# Life Is A Circle

*Mary Ann Fusco* © 1984
*Recorded on* Aradia's Song For All Seasons

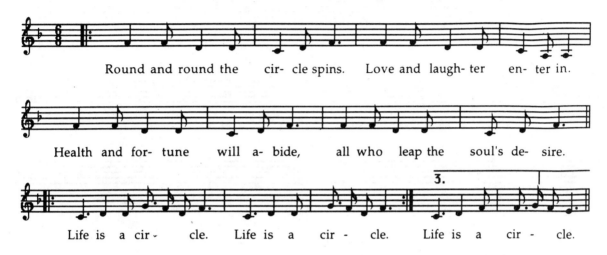

Round and round the cir- cle spins. Love and laugh- ter en- ter in.

Health and for- tune will a- bide, all who leap the soul's de- sire.

Life is a cir - cle. Life is a cir - cle. Life is a cir - cle.

# Round We Go

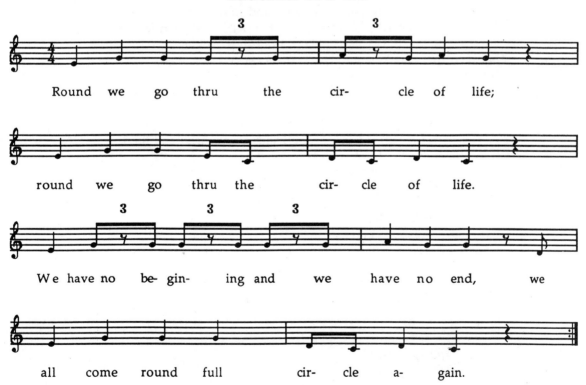

Round we go thru the cir- cle of life;

round we go thru the cir- cle of life.

We have no be- gin- ing and we have no end, we

all come round full cir- cle a- gain.

# Celtic Goddess Blessing

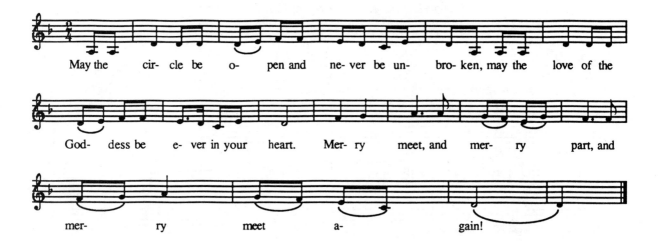

May the cir- cle be o- pen and ne- ver be un- bro- ken, may the love of the
God- dess be e- ver in your heart. Mer- ry meet, and mer- ry part, and
mer- ry meet a- gain!

**Dance:**

Divide group into equal numbers with partners. All stand in a circle facing in. The partner on the left side of the couple will be moving, while the other partner stays still.

**May the circle be open**

The moving partner releases his/her left hand from circle (right hand is holding partner's hand) and moves into the circle facing partner and giving him/her left hand. Partners are standing face to face and holding both hands, making a circle between them, looking into each others eyes.

**but unbroken.**

Gently separate hands, opening palms to each other, feeling energy still flowing between you.

**May the love of the Goddess be ever in your heart**

Look into your partner's eyes, raise hands above head and then bring them slowly down over your heart.

**Merry meet and merry part**

Hug partner on each side of cheek.

**And merry meet again**

Leave each other. The moving person releases his/her partner's left hand and moves back into the larger circle extending their right hand to their neighbor who will become their next partner.

# The Circle is Open

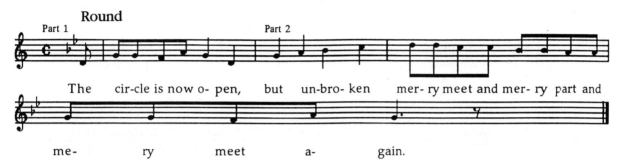

Round

Part 1    Part 2

The cir-cle is now o- pen, but un-bro- ken mer- ry meet and mer- ry part and

me- ry meet a- gain.

# Go in Beauty

*William Baker*
*Recorded on* Path of the Heart

Go in beau- ty peace be with you till we

meet in our hearts in the light.

**Dance:**
Stand face to face with a partner for each cycle and then move on to a new partner. Feel free to improvise.

**1. Go in Beauty**
Look into each other's eyes, raise arms and hands and bring them down and around partner's body in a motion of blessing and healing, caressing their aura

**2. Peace be with you**
Hold hands, looking into each other's eyes.

**3. Till we meet with our hearts**
Put your hands over your heart, experiencing deep love and heart connection with your partner.

**4. In the light**
Radiate arms and hands outward, feeling yourself surrounded in light.

# Kwaheri

*Traditional African Chant from Kenya and Tanzania*
*Recorded on* The Fire Within *by Libana,* 1990

This is a popular good-bye song often sung at the end of parties and gatherings. Translation: 'Goodbye, dear friend. We will meet again if God wills'.

Kwa he- ri, kwa- he- ri, m- pen- zi kwa- he- ri, kwa-

he- ri, tu- ta- o- na- na te- na tu- ki- ja- ri- wa.

# May the Long Time Sunshine

*Words by Robin Williamson Music by Yogi Bhajan*
*Recorded by* The Incredible String Band *in the 60's*

May the long time sun shine up- on you. All love sur- round

you. And the pure light with- in you guide your way home.

**Verse:**
A Goddess version with words by Z Budapest. Substitute other
Goddess names.
May Artemis protect you
And Hera Provide you
And the Womansoul within you
Guide your way home
**Dance:**
Stand face to face with a partner for each cycle and then move on
to new partner. Improvise movements for each line.

# Appendices

## Illustrations

By Jan Billings
New Avalonia Designs
19a West End Street
Glastonbury,Somerset BA 16,
except for the following:
 1. All the diagrams and the illustrations on pp.
16, 23, 46, 61, 71, 92, 97, 121, 146, 147, 149,
152, 173 & 260 by Jeanette Gawry Perman.
 2. p. 105; Snake Goddess, Reproduction of
drawing by Laurelin Remington-Wolf from
*Shakti Woman,* by Vicki Noble fig. 12B, p 35,
Used by Permission.

3. p. 117; Peruvian Pacha Mama. Reproduction
of drawing by Laurelin Remington-Wolf from
*Shakti Woman,* by Vicki Noble Fig. 17 p. 57.
Used by permission.
4. p. 238; Drawing by Wahid Shiloh.
5. p. 211; Heart Drawing by Francois Monnet.
6. p.168; From a Mexican block print drawing of Quetalcoatl. Source unknown.

## Index of meditations and rituals used in the book

# Sources for recordings and chants used in this book

Lisa Thiel
Sacred Dream Productions
6336 N. Oracle Rd.
Suite 326-307
Tucson, AZ
*Songs of the Spirit; Prayers for the Planet;*
*Songs of Transformation; Rising of the Phoe-*
*nix; Lady of the Lake*

Out Front Music
Charlie Murphy
P.O. Box 12188
Seattle, WA 98102
(206) 547-4525
*Catch the Fire; Canticles of Light*

David Casselman
254 Clinton Pk.
San Francisco, CA 94103
*Sanctify The Earth*

Rabbi Nathan L. Segal
220 Redwood Hwy. #118
Mill Valley, CA 94941
*Joseph and Nathan* ©1968

The Bear Tribe Medicine Society
P.O. Box 9167
Spokane, WA 99209
*The Dawning—Chants of the*
*Medicine Wheel;*
*Coming Light—Chants to Honor the Earth*
*Mother*

Karen Beth
Catkin Music
Box 371
Bearsville, NY 12409
*Each One of Us*

Libana, Inc.
Box 530
Cambridge, MA 02140
*A Circle is Cast; Fire Within*

Jim Berenholtz
231A Fairview Street
Laguna Beach, CA 92631
*Turquoise Waters*

Prana
Tangelynen, CWM COU
Newcastle Emlyn
Dyfed SA 389PQ Wales
*First Chants; Second Chants; Seven Seasons*
*Suns, Rocks, Stones and Crystals;*
*Return of the Mayflower*

Michael Stillwater
Inner Harmony
P.O. Box 1087
Capitola, CA 95010
*You Belong to Love; Voices of theHeart; One*
*Light; Celebration;*
*Set Your Heartsong Free; Wings of Prayer*

Mary Ann Fusco/Aradia
Moonwise Music
720 S. 44th Street
Boulder, CO 80303
*Songs for All Seasons*

Susan Elizabeth Hale
P.O. Box 777
Sandia Park, NM 87047
*Circle the Earth With Song*

Shekhinah Mountainwater
305 Effey
Santa Cruz, CA 95063
*Songs and Chants of the Goddess*

Joyful Sound/Joy Chappell
2010 S. Broadway
Pittsburgh, KS 66762
*The Connection, Babaji, Peace*
*Anthem*

Starhawk and Reclaiming Community
P.O. Box 14404
San Francisco, CA 94114
*Chants/Ritual Music; Let it Begin Now*

Kiva
P.O. Box 0403
Rockville, MD 20848
*Renewal; Alchemy; The Healing Art*

Mother Tongue
EarthSpirit Community
P.O. Box 365
Medford, MA 02155
*Tribal Drums; All Beings of The Earth; Fire*
*Dance*

Earthsong Productions
Anne Williams
P.O. Box 780
Sedona, AZ 86336
*Summer Rose; Song of Isis; The Song of the*
*Jaguar; Children of the Sun*

Abbi Spinner and J. Magnus McBride
Tobias Beckwith & Assoc.
305 W. 52nd Street
New York, NY 10019
*Spinner and Magnus—Songs from the Center*
*of the Sacred Circle*

Michael Tierra
Box 712
Santa Cruz, CA 95061

Jonathan Goldman/Spirit Sounds, Inc.
Box 2240
Boulder, CO 80306
*Gateways—Men's Drumming and Chanting*

Rick Hamouris/Buffalo
Forever Forests
P.O. Box 212
Redwood Valley, CA 95470
*Welcome to Annwfn*

The Ojai Foundation
Box 1620
Ojai, CA 93023
*The Giveaway; The Circle*

Terry Dash
22 Varnum St.
Arlington, MA 02179

Susan Arrow and the Quivers
North Bear Music
P.O. Box 6404
Portland, OR 97228
*Welcome Sweet Pleasure*

David Eply/Sage Medicine Heart
#9 Via Poka
Carmel Valley, CA 93924

Acoustic Medicine
2462 Matilija Canyon
Ojai, CA 93023
*Uplifting the World; Return of the Circle*

Adele Getty
RR1 Box 123a
Santa Fe, NM 87505

Silver Branch Productions
c/o Flat One
64 High Street
Glastonbury, England
*Eye of the Aeon*

David Zeller
c/o Tara Publishers
Vel Pasternak
29 Derby Ave.
Cedarhurst, NY 11516
*Path of the Heart; Ruach/Spirit; Let Go*

Lia Argo
*Heartsongs*
105 Simcoe
Victoria, BC VBVIKS Canada

Dolphinsong Unlimited
Alicia Bonnet
Box 1403
Mt. Shasta, CA 96067
*Opening; Trusting*

W. A. Mathieu
9195 Barnett Valley Rd.
Sebastopol, CA 95472

Robin Van Liew
1507 E. Franklin St. #362
Chapel Hill, NC 27514
*Native American Ceremonial Chants*
(Distributed by Sacred Spirit Music, Box 300,
New Lebanon, NY 12125)

Robert Gass—On Wings of Song
Spring Hill Music
P.O. Box 800
Boulder, CO 80306
Extended chant tape series. Tapes include: *From*
*the Goddess; Alleluya; Hara Hara; Om Nama*
*Shivaya; Kalama—The Sufi Song of Love;*
*Medicine Wheel; Shri Ram.*

Sarah Pirtle
The Discovery Center
P.O. Box 28, Buckland MA 01330
*Two Hands Hold the Earth; The Wind is Telling*
*Secrets; Magical Earth*

# Recommended Tapes

*Journeys in Sound and Healing*
Kate Marks
Box 428
Amherst, MA 01004

Harmony Network
Brooke Medicine Eagle(Many chant tapes)
Box 2550
Guerneville, CA 95446

*Colorado Midwife Tape*
Box 106
Boulder, CO 80302

*Songs to the Goddess*
c/o Sonoma County Birth Network
Box 1005
Occidental, CA 95465

*Cosmic Chants*
Paramahansa Yogananda
Self Realization Fellowship
3880 San Rafael
Los Angeles, CA 90065

*Sounds of the Sacred—Chants of Love and Prayer ( 3 Tapes and Songbook)*
Kripalu - by - Mail
Kripalu Center
Box 793
Lenox, MA 01240

# Recommended Books

**Self—Transformation through Music**
Joanne Crandall,
Quest Books

**Sound Medicine**
Leah Maggie Garfield
Celestial Arts
Berkeley, CA

**Toning**
Laurel Elizabeth Keyes
De Vorss & Co.

**Sound Health**
Steven Halpern
Harper and Row

**Sounding the Inner Landscape—Music as Medicine**
Kay Gardner
Caduceus Publications
Box 27
Stonington. ME 04681

**Healing Sounds—The Power of Harmonics**
Jonathan Goldman
Element Books

**The Healing Voice—Traditional and Contemporary Toning, Chanting and Singing**
Joy Gardner-Gordon
The Crossing Press
Freedom, CA 95019

**The Book of Sound Therapy—Heal Yourself with Music and Voice**
Olivia Dewhurst—Maddock
Simon and Schuster

**Freeing the Natural Voice**
Kristin Linklater
Drama Book Publishers

**Music and Sound in the Healing Arts**
John Beaulieu
Station Hill Press

**The Mysticism of Sound**
Hazrat Inayat Khan
Omega Press
Box 1030 D
New Lebanon,N.Y

**The Circle of Life—Rituals from the Human Family**
Arthur Davidson
Harper San Francisco

**Rituals For Our Times—Celebrating, Healing and Changing our Lives and Relationships**
Evan Imber-Black and Janine Roberts
Harper Collins

**The Power of Myth** (and many others)
Joseph Campbell
Doubleday, N.Y

**Ceremonial Circle—Practice, Ritual and Renewal for Personal and Community Healing**
Sedonia Cahill and Joshua Halpern
Harper/ Collins

**Women's Rituals**
Barbara Walker
Harper and Row

**Ceremonies for Change—Creating Personal Ritual to Heal Life's Hurts**
Lynda S. Paladin
Stillpoint Publishing

**Celebrating Life—Rites of Passage for all ages**
Tziporah Klein
Delphi Press

**The Spiral Dance**
Starhawk
Harper and Row

**The Language of the Goddess— Unearthing the Hidden Symbols of Western Civilization**
Marija Gimbutas
Harper San Francisco

**The Book of Goddesses and Heroines**
Patricia Monaghan
Dutton, N.Y.

**The Goddess Celebrates—Anthology of Women's Rituals**
Ed. by Diane Stein
The Crossing Press
Freedom,CA.

**Shakti Woman—The New Female Shamanism**
Vicki Noble
Harper San Francisco

**The Way of the Shaman**
Michael Harner
Bantam Books
Also drumming tapes available for shamanic journeys.

**The Medicine Wheel—Earth Astrology**
SunBear and Wabun
Prentice Hall
Englewood Cliffs, NJ 07632

**Medicine Cards—The Discovery of Power Through the Ways of Animals**
Jamie Sams & David Carson
Bear & Co., Santa Fe, NM

**Animal Energies**
Gary Buffalo Horn Man and Sherry Firedancer
Dancing Otter Publishing
PO Box 9709
Spokane, WA 99209

**Wingspan—Inside the Men's Movement**
Christopher Harding, editor
St Martin's Press
See also: **Wingspan, Journal of the Male Spirit**, a quarterly
Box 23550
Brightmoor Station
Detroit, MI 48223

**Circle of Men**
Bill Kauth
St. Martin's Press

# Songbooks

**Songs of the Earth—
Music of the World**
Anna Kealoha
Celestial Arts
P.O. Box 7327
Berkeley, CA 94707

**Sounds of the Sacred—Chants of Love
and Prayer** (Hindu chants)
Kripalu Center
Box 793
Lenox, MA 01240

**Circle Song Book**
Yaffa Rosenthal
Box 574
Trinidad, CA 95570

**The Green Earth Spirituality Songbook**
Jesse E. Shoup, G.W.
Box 764
Boonville, CA 95415

**One Earth Songbook**
Sunrise Press
Box 2920
Wellington, New Zealand
ISBN 0-9597840-0-4

**Sacred Canons; 101 Rounds
for Singing**
World Around Songs
Rt 5, Box 398
Burnsville, N.C 28714
  (704) 675- 5343

**For the Beauty of the Earth—Environmen-
tal Songbook**
Hudson River Clearwater
Folk Project
Box 41
Mendham, N J 07945

**Rise Up Singing**
Edited by Peter Blood & Annie Patterson
A Sing Out Corp. Publicatio
Box 5253
Bethlehem, PA 18015

**Libana Songbook**
Box 530
Cambridge, MA 02140

# New Age and Sacred Music Distributors

Heartsong Review
(Quarterly catalog with many titles)
Resource Guide for New Age
Music of the Spirit
P.O. Box 1084
Cottage Grove, OR 97424

New Leaf Distributing Company
5425 Tulane Drive, SW
Atlanta, GA 30336

Music Design
Wholesale catalog of music, videos, books, children's music
207 East Buffalo Street
Milwaukee, WI 53202

Ladyslipper Catalog
Recordings by Women
P.0. Box 3124-R
Durham, NC 27715

Sacred Spirit Music
RD1 Box 1030D
New Lebanon, NY 12125

# Drumming Resources

Mickey Hart
**Drumming at the Edge of Magic
A Journey into the Spirit of Percussion**
Harper Collins
(Book and audio cassette tapes)

Foundation for Shamanic Studies
Box 670
Norwalk, CT 06852
(Drumming tapes for shamanic journeys)

Earth Drum Council
P.O. Box 184
Concord, MA O1742
(Organization which offers regular drumming cir-
  cles and camps through-out the year on the East
  coast.)

  Makhan Burt (Ceramic dumbeks)
   4500 19th St. #379
   Boulder CO 80304

Tom Bickford
1379 South East Street
Amherst, MA 01002 (Drumaker)

# Music and Dance Organizations

Institute for Music Health and Education
P.O. Box 1244
Boulder, CO 80306

Circle Dance Network/England
Janet Savage
31 Castle Roda
Colchester
COI IUW, U. K.

Circle Dance Network/U.S.A
Touchstone Farm
132 West St
Easthampton, MA 01027

Sound Healers Association
P.O. Box 2240
Boulder, CO 80306

Music for People
7 Middletown Rd.
Roxbury, New Hampshire 03431
(603) 352-4941
(Network of people interested in music improvisation)

# Index of Titles

# Chant Reference Charts

| Contemporary | Ch | P | MF | D | CH |
|---|---|---|---|---|---|
| Temple Round | 1 | 4 | R | | |
| God of Beauty | 1 | 4 | 1 | | |
| O Great Spirit | 1 | 6 | 1 | | • |
| Spirit is Around Us | 1 | 6 | 1 | | • |
| Archangel Invocation | 1 | 8 | 1 | | |
| Power, Power, We Are Calling | 1 | 8 | 1 | | |
| We Are the Power in Everyone | 1 | 9 | 1 | | |
| We are Alive | 1 | 12 | 1 | | |
| Holy Vision | 1 | 13 | 1 | | |
| Dreamtime | 1 | 14 | 1 | | |
| Behold a Sacred Voice | 1 | 14 | R,M | | |
| Invocation to the Four Directions | 1 | 19 | 1 | | |
| Song to the Four Directions | 1 | 20 | 1 | | |
| Spirit Invocation | 1 | 21 | 1 | | • |
| Call to Spirit - Invocation Song | 1 | 21 | 1 | | |
| Four Winds Blessing | 1 | 22 | 1 | | |
| Turn to the Mountain | 2 | 28 | 1 | | |
| We Are One With the Soul of the Earth | 2 | 29 | 2 | • | |
| See the Earth is Turning | 2 | 30 | 1 | | |
| Round and Round | 2 | 30 | R | • | • |
| Ocean Mother | 2 | 32 | 2 | | • |
| The Ocean is the Beginning of the Earth | 2 | 32 | 2 | | • |
| Born of Water | 2 | 33 | R | | |
| The River is Flowing (Spanish) | 2 | 34 | 1 | • | |
| Fire Flow Free | 2 | 37 | 1 | | • |
| Step into the Holy Fire | 2 | 37 | 1 | | |
| Rise With the Fire | 2 | 38 | 1 | | |
| Firechild | 2 | 38 | 1 | | • |
| Fire of the Heart | 2 | 40 | 1 | | |
| The Sun Goes Up | 2 | 43 | 1 | | • |
| Burning Fire Lights the Sun | 2 | 44 | R | | • |
| Come, Children, Come to the Radiant Sun | 2 | 44 | 1 | • | • |
| Woke Up This Morning | 2 | 45 | 1 | | • |
| Pure White Light | 2 | 46 | 1 | | |
| Be a Living Light | 2 | 47 | R | | • |
| Light is Returning | 2 | 48 | 1 | • | |
| All the Air is Sacred | 2 | 51 | 1 | | • |
| Tall Trees, Warm Fire | 2 | 54 | R | | • |
| Air I Am | 2 | 54 | 1 | | • |
| Earth and Ocean | 2 | 55 | R | | • |

### Key to Musical Forms

R——Round    C——Counterpoint
1——One Part    M——Multipart
2——Two Part    CR——Call and Response

### Key to Charts

Ch——Chapter    MF——Musical Form
P——Page    D——Dance
CH——Good for Children

| Contemporary, cont'd. | Ch | P | MF | D | CH |
|---|---|---|---|---|---|
| Air Moves Us | 2 | 55 | 1 | • | • |
| Deep Deep You Are | 2 | 56 | 1 | | |
| Spirit of the Wind | 2 | 57 | 1 | | |
| Fire and Air | 2 | 58 | 1 | | |
| Earth My Body, Water My Blood | 2 | 59 | R | • | • |
| I Am Becoming You | 2 | 60 | M | | |
| Rainbow Circle | 3 | 64 | 1 | | • |
| Morning Turns to Glory | 3 | 65 | R | | • |
| Evening Breeze | 3 | 65 | R | | • |
| Spirits Flying in the Sky | 3 | 66 | 1 | | |
| Earth Child, Star Child | 3 | 67 | 1 | | |
| Mother I Feel You Under My Feet | 3 | 69 | 1 | • | • |
| Two Hands Hold the Earth | 3 | 70 | 1 | • | |
| Life is Like a Crystal in the Sun | 3 | 72 | 1 | | • |
| The Rocks, the Stones and the Crystals | 3 | 72 | 1 | | • |
| I Am the Spirit of the Tree | 3 | 74 | 1 | | • |
| The Spirit of the Plant | 3 | 74 | 1 | | |
| My Roots Go Down | 3 | 75 | 1 | | • |
| In the Garden | 3 | 77 | 1 | | • |
| Fur and Feathers | 3 | 79 | 1 | | • |
| Buffalo | 3 | 81 | 1 | | • |
| White Dolphin Swimming | 3 | 82 | 1 | | • |
| Epona–Song to the White Horse Goddess | 3 | 83 | 1 | | |
| Be a Butterfly | 3 | 84 | 1 | | • |
| Condor Song | 3 | 85 | 1 | | |
| Spinning Around The Wheel | 3 | 85 | 1 | | • |
| Owl Song | 3 | 87 | 1 | | • |
| I Circle Around | 3 | 88 | 1 | • | • |
| We All Fly Like Eagles | 3 | 89 | CR | • | • |
| We Are an Old People | 3 | 91 | 1,C | • | |
| Blood of the Ancients | 3 | 92 | 1 | • | |
| Come Forward and Meet Us | 3 | 93 | 1 | | |
| We Ask the Ancient Women | 3 | 94 | 1 | | |
| To the Old Man / Woman of Creation | 3 | 94 | 1 | | |
| Ancestors | 3 | 95 | 1 | | |
| Woman am I | 4 | 100 | 1 | | |
| Blessed is She | 4 | 101 | 1 | | |
| Woman Am I # 2 | 4 | 101 | 1 | | |
| Snake Woman | 4 | 104 | 1, CR | • | |
| White Buffalo Woman | 4 | 106 | 1 | | |
| We are Changers | 4 | 107 | 2,C | | |
| She Changes Everything She Touches | 4 | 107 | 1,C | | |
| Kore's Chant | 4 | 108 | 1 | | |
| Changing Woman | 4 | 109 | 1 | | |
| We are the Flow, We are the Ebb | 4 | 110 | 1 | • | |
| Grandmother Spider Woman | 4 | 110 | 1 | | • |

| Contemporary, cont'd. | Ch | P | MF | D | CH |
|---|---|---|---|---|---|
| Lady Weave Your Circle Tight | 4 | 111 | R | • | |
| Spiralling into the Center | 4 | 111 | 1, C | • | |
| Sure as the Wind | 4 | 112 | R | | |
| We Are Sisters On A Journey | 4 | 113 | 1 | • | |
| A Circle of Women | 4 | 114 | 1 | | |
| River of Birds | 4 | 116 | M | | |
| Ancient Mother | 4 | 117 | 1 | | |
| Mother of All Things | 4 | 118 | 1 | | |
| Return to the Mother | 4 | 118 | 1 | | |
| Take your Gifts Mother | 4 | 119 | 1 | | |
| Sacred Corn Mother | 4 | 120 | 1 | | |
| She is Bountiful, She is Beautiful | 4 | 120 | 1 | | |
| Source to Source | 4 | 122 | 1 | | |
| Mine is the Blood | 4 | 122 | 1 | | |
| Bless The Shining Children | 4 | 125 | 1 | | • |
| Keep Breathing | 4 | 125 | 1 | | |
| We Wish You A Happy Birthday | 4 | 126 | R | | • |
| You Are a Hollow Bamboo | 4 | 127 | 1 | | |
| In Balance With the Moon | 4 | 127 | 1 | | |
| By A Woman | 4 | 127 | R | | |
| Welcome Little One | 4 | 128 | 1 | | |
| Isis Astarte Diana | 4 | 134 | 1, C | • | |
| Isis, Heart of the Mountain | 4 | 135 | 1 | | |
| Alma Hina | 4 | 136 | 1 | | |
| The Moon is my Mistress | 4 | 143 | 1 | | |
| We are In Tune with the Healing of the Moon | 4 | 144 | 1 | | |
| Diana, Your Children Call | 4 | 148 | 1 | | |
| Into the Silence of the Night | 4 | 148 | 1 | | |
| Full Moonlight Dance | 4 | 150 | R | | |
| Moon Mother | 4 | 150 | 1 | | |
| Luna's Lullaby | 4 | 151 | 1 | | |
| Triple Goddess Chant | 4 | 154 | 1 | | |
| She's Been Waiting | 4 | 155 | 1 | | |
| Mother Goddess Keep Me Whole | 4 | 156 | 1 | | |
| Quetzalcoatl | 5 | 168 | 2 | | |
| Thoth, Hermes, Mercury | 5 | 169 | 1 | | |
| Look into the Fire | 5 | 172 | R | | |
| Shiva Dance Dance Dance | 5 | 173 | 1 | • | |
| Prayer of St. Francis | 5 | 182 | M | | |
| La Illaha II Allah Hu | 5 | 186 | 1 | | |
| All I Really Want | 5 | 188 | 1 | | • |
| Everything Hurt is Healed Again | 6 | 194 | 1 | | |
| Purify and Heal Us | 6 | 195 | 1 | | |
| Wash Away My Tears | 6 | 195 | 1 | | • |
| When I Let Go of Fear | 6 | 195 | 1 | | • |
| I Am A Circle, I am Healing You | 6 | 196 | 1, CR | • | • |

| Contemporary, cont'd. | Ch | P | MF | D | CH |
|---|---|---|---|---|---|
| Dark is the Path Alone | 6 | 198 | R | | |
| Healing By Night | 6 | 198 | 1 | | |
| I Will Not Be Afraid | 6 | 199 | 1 | | • |
| All Beings Of the Earth | 6 | 200 | 2 | | |
| I Will be Gentle with Myself | 6 | 201 | 1 | | • |
| Give Me A Little Sunshine | 6 | 202 | 1 | | • |
| Giving Birth to Myself | 6 | 202 | 1 | | |
| So Beautiful | 6 | 204 | 1 | | • |
| You are Beautiful | 6 | 204 | 1 | | • |
| All Shall Be Well | 6 | 205 | 1 | | • |
| We Love Your Love | 6 | 205 | 1 | | • |
| Love is the Only Power | 6 | 206 | 1 | • | • |
| Listen, Listen, Listen | 6 | 208 | 1 | | • |
| Start the Day with Love (Traditional) | 6 | 208 | R | | • |
| I Surrender To Love | 6 | 209 | 2 | | |
| There's Only One Lover | 6 | 210 | 1 | | |
| Let My Heart Fly Open | 6 | 211 | 1 | | |
| Share Your Love | 6 | 212 | M | | |
| From You I Receive | 6 | 213 | 1 | | • |
| Our Magic is Our Giveaway | 6 | 214 | 1 | | • |
| The Circle Shapes Us | 6 | 218 | 1 | | • |
| All Knowing Spirit Within Me | 6 | 218 | R | | • |
| Holy Spirit Within | 7 | 219 | 2 | • | |
| I Am As God Created Me | 7 | 220 | M | | |
| I Am | 7 | 222 | 1 | | • |
| There's a Man / Woman in You | 7 | 228 | 1 | | • |
| I am One With the Heart of the Mother/ Father | 7 | 229 | M | | |
| You Are My Mother/Father | 7 | 230 | 1 | | • |
| Under the Sky | 7 | 240 | R | | • |
| Light a Candle For Peace | 7 | 242 | 1 | | • |
| I Love the People | 7 | 243 | 1 | | • |
| May All Beings Be Well | 7 | 244 | 1 | | • |
| Peace on Earth | 7 | 244 | 2 | | • |
| Sanctify the Earth | 7 | 245 | 1 | | |
| Peace Be To You | 7 | 246 | M | | |
| Thank You for This Day | 7 | 252 | 1 | | • |
| Let us Give Thanks | 7 | 253 | R | | • |
| Thank You Mother Earth | 7 | 253 | 1 | | • |
| We Are a Circle Within a Circle | 7 | 257 | 2 | • | • |
| Round We Go | 7 | 259 | 1 | | • |
| Life is a Circle | 7 | 259 | 1, C | | |
| Go in Beauty | 7 | 261 | 1 | • | • |
| May the Long Time Sunshine | 7 | 262 | 1 | • | • |

| Native American | Ch | P | MF | D | CH |
|---|---|---|---|---|---|
| Now I Walk in Beauty | 1 | 5 | R | • | • |
| Where I Sit is Holy | 1 | 5 | 1 | | • |
| Spirit is Around Us | 1 | 6 | 1 | | • |
| Wani Wachialo—Wakan Tanka | 1 | 9 | 1 | | |
| Hey Ungawa | 1 | 10 | 1 | | • |
| Apache Power Chant | 1 | 12 | 1 | | |
| Holy Vision | 1 | 13 | 1 | | |
| Behold a Sacred Voice | 1 | 14 | R,M | | |
| Song to the Four Directions | 1 | 20 | 1 | | |
| The Earth is Our Mother | 2 | 27 | 1 | • | • |
| Wichitai Tai | 2 | 33 | 1 | | • |
| Firechild | 2 | 38 | 1 | | • |
| Cree Sunrise Song | 2 | 42 | 1 | | |
| Zuni Sunrise Song | 2 | 42 | 1 | | |
| Kuate Leno Leno | 2 | 43 | 1 | | • |
| The Dawning of a New Day | 2 | 49 | 1 | | |
| Soaring Like the Wind | 2 | 51 | 1 | | • |
| The Earth, The Water, The Fire, The Air | 2 | 53 | 1 | • | • |
| Makowele | 2 | 58 | 1 | | |
| Look at the Beauty | 3 | 64 | 1 | | • |
| Sing a Song of the Earth/Sky | 3 | 68 | 2 | | |
| Mother I Feel You Under My Feet | 3 | 69 | 1 | • | • |
| Hinamay-Acorn Grinding Song | 3 | 76 | 1 | | |
| Shewin Shewiliga | 3 | 77 | 1 | | |
| Ka Yo—Song of the Bear | 3 | 79 | 1 | | • |
| Ya Na Ho | 3 | 80 | 1 | | • |
| Najoli Win—Grandfather Bear | 3 | 80 | 1 | | • |
| Hey Ye Ye | 3 | 81 | 1 | • | • |
| Heya Heya Weya | 3 | 81 | 1 | | • |
| Little Deer Song | 3 | 83 | 1 | | |
| Wendeya Ho | 3 | 84 | 1 | | • |
| Spinning Around The Wheel | 3 | 85 | 1 | | • |
| Blue Heron Song | 3 | 86 | 1 | | |
| I Circle Around | 3 | 88 | 1 | • | • |
| Weyniya | 3 | 88 | 1 | | |
| We All Fly Like Eagles | 3 | 89 | CR | • | • |
| O Grandmother, I Feel You Lift Me Up | 3 | 95 | 1 | • | |
| O Grandmother, We are Calling to You | 3 | 96 | 1 | | |
| Wey O Wey, Grandmother | 3 | 96 | 1 | • | |
| Yana Wana Yana | 4 | 102 | 1 | | |
| White Buffalo Woman | 4 | 106 | 1 | | |
| Sacred Corn Mother | 4 | 120 | 1 | | |
| Willow Song ( Sha Noon) | 4 | 123 | 1 | | |
| Yani Yoni Ya Hu Way Hey | 4 | 124 | 1 | | |
| Eni Wichi Chayo | 4 | 128 | 1 | | |
| Neesa | 4 | 143 | R | | • |

| Native American, cont'd. | Ch | P | MF | D | CH |
|---|---|---|---|---|---|
| Hay Ya Hay Ya—Moon Song | 4 | 144 | 1 | | • |
| Grandmother Moon | 4 | 145 | 1 | | |
| Into the Silence of the Night | 4 | 148 | 1 | | |
| Ya No Ah | 7 | 223 | 1 | • | • |
| My Words Are Tied in One | 7 | 224 | 1 | | • |
| Wehnahani Yo | 7 | 240 | 1 | • | |
| Thank You for This Day | 7 | 252 | 1 | | • |

| Pagan | Ch | P | MF | D | CH |
|---|---|---|---|---|---|
| A Circle is Cast | 1 | 18 | M | | |
| Spirit Invocation | 1 | 21 | 1 | | • |
| Call to Spirit - Invocation Song | 1 | 21 | 1 | | |
| Air I Am | 2 | 54 | 1 | | • |
| Air Moves Us | 2 | 55 | 1 | • | • |
| We Are an Old People | 3 | 91 | 1,C | • | |
| Blood of the Ancients | 3 | 92 | 1 | • | |
| The Witch Song | 4 | 103 | 1 | | |
| Snake Woman | 4 | 104 | 1, CR | • | |
| We are Changers | 4 | 107 | 2,C | | |
| She Changes Everything She Touches | 4 | 107 | 1,C | | |
| Kore's Chant | 4 | 108 | 1 | | |
| Changing Woman | 4 | 109 | 1 | | |
| We are the Flow, We are the Ebb | 4 | 110 | 1 | • | |
| Grandmother Spider Woman | 4 | 110 | 1 | | • |
| Lady Weave Your Circle Tight | 4 | 111 | R | • | |
| Spiralling into the Center | 4 | 111 | 1, C | • | |
| A Circle of Women | 4 | 114 | 1 | | |
| Return to the Mother | 4 | 118 | 1 | | |
| She is Bountiful, She is Beautiful | 4 | 120 | 1 | | |
| By A Woman | 4 | 127 | R | | |
| Opening Up | 4 | 130 | R | • | |
| We All Come from the Goddess | 4 | 131 | 1, C | • | • |
| The Goddess is Alive | 4 | 132 | 1 | | • |
| Children of the Goddess | 4 | 132 | 1 | | • |
| Goddess of Life | 4 | 133 | M | | |
| Isis Astarte Diana | 4 | 134 | 1, C | • | |
| Isis, Heart of the Mountain | 4 | 135 | 1 | | |
| Alma Hina | 4 | 136 | 1 | | |
| O Brighde | 4 | 140 | 1 | | |
| Into the Silence of the Night | 4 | 148 | 1 | | |
| Hecate,Cerridwen | 4 | 153 | 1 | | |
| Crone and Sage | 4 | 153 | 1, C | | |
| Triple Goddess Chant | 4 | 154 | 1 | | |

## Pagan, cont'd.

| | Ch | P | MF | D | CH |
|---|---|---|---|---|---|
| She's Been Waiting | 4 | 155 | 1 | | |
| Mother, Maiden, Crone in Me | 4 | 156 | 1 | | |
| Mother Goddess Keep Me Whole | 4 | 156 | 1 | | |
| Male I Am | 5 | 160 | 1 | | |
| Horned One, Lover, Son | 5 | 162 | 1 | | |
| Cernunnos | 5 | 163 | 1 | | |
| Herne | 5 | 163 | 1 | | |
| Hoof and Horn | 5 | 164 | 1, C | • | |
| Mithra Osiris | 5 | 165 | 1, C | | |
| We All Come From The Sun God | 5 | 166 | 1, C | • | • |
| Pan, Wotan, Baphomet | 5 | 166 | 1, C | • | |
| Green God | 5 | 167 | 1, CR | | • |
| Thoth, Hermes, Mercury | 5 | 169 | 1 | | |
| Come to Us | 5 | 169 | 1 | | |
| Praise Unto the God and Goddess | 7 | 255 | R | | |
| We Are a Circle Within a Circle | 7 | 257 | 2 | • | • |
| No End to the Circle | 7 | 258 | 1 | | • |
| Round We Go | 7 | 259 | 1 | | • |
| Life is a Circle | 7 | 259 | 1, C | | |
| Celtic Goddess Blessing | 7 | 260 | 1 | • | • |
| The Circle is Open | 7 | 261 | R | | |

## Christian

| | Ch | P | MF | D | CH |
|---|---|---|---|---|---|
| Rise Up O Flame | 2 | 39 | R | | • |
| Woke Up This Morning | 2 | 45 | 1 | | • |
| This Little Light | 2 | 47 | 1 | | • |
| Opening Up | 4 | 130 | R | • | |
| Jesus Loves the Little Children | 5 | 178 | 1 | | • |
| Jubilate Deo | 5 | 178 | R | | |
| Kyrie | 5 | 179 | M | | |
| Surrexit Christe | 5 | 179 | R | | |
| Lord of the Dance | 5 | 180 | 1 | | |
| Te Ariki | 5 | 181 | 1 | | |
| Prayer of St. Francis | 5 | 182 | M | | |
| Fellowship | 5 | 190 | R | | |
| Yes, God is Real | 7 | 221 | 1 | | |
| Sing Together | 7 | 233 | R | | • |
| Praise Ye the Lord With Joy | 7 | 234 | 1 | | • |
| Rock' A My Soul | 7 | 235 | 1 | | • |
| Sing And Rejoice | 7 | 236 | R | | • |
| Won' t You Rock Us | 7 | 236 | 1 | | • |
| Alleluya/Glory | 7 | 237 | 2 | | |
| Rejoice in the Lord | 7 | 237 | R | | • |
| We Are One in the Spirit | 7 | 239 | 1 | | • |

## Christian, cont'd.

| | Ch | P | MF | D | CH |
|---|---|---|---|---|---|
| Da Pacem | 7 | 251 | R | | |
| Dona Nobis Pacem | 7 | 251 | R | | |
| Tallis Canon | 7 | 254 | M | | |
| Thank You For the World | 7 | 254 | 1 | | • |
| For Health and Strength | 7 | 255 | R | | • |

## Sufi/Islamic

| | Ch | P | MF | D | CH |
|---|---|---|---|---|---|
| Wazifa Canon | 5 | 185 | M | | |
| La Illaha Il Allah Hu | 5 | 186 | 1 | | |
| Ikhlas Sura | 5 | 186 | 1 | | |
| O Thou Sustainer | 7 | 255 | 1 | | • |

## Jewish

| | Ch | P | MF | D | CH |
|---|---|---|---|---|---|
| Eliyahu | 5 | 184 | 1 | | |
| Ano Ki Shemain | 5 | 184 | 1 | | |
| Return Again | 7 | 225 | 1 | • | |
| Hida | 7 | 233 | R | | • |
| Nigun | 7 | 234 | 1 | • | • |
| Vine and Fig Tree | 7 | 243 | R | | • |
| Shabbat Shalom | 7 | 249 | 1 | | • |
| Havenu Shalom | 7 | 250 | 1 | • | |

## Hindu

| | Ch | P | MF | D | CH |
|---|---|---|---|---|---|
| Ganga Ki Jai Jai | 2 | 34 | 1 | • | |
| My Divine Mother | 4 | 119 | 1 | | |
| Kali Durga | 4 | 137 | 1 | | |
| Hindu Goddess Chant | 4 | 138 | 1 | | |
| Hare Krishna | 5 | 170 | 1 | | • |
| Sri Ram | 5 | 170 | 1 | | • |
| Om Nama Shivaya #1 | 5 | 171 | 1 | • | • |
| Gopala | 5 | 171 | 1 | | • |
| Om Nama Shivaya #2 | 5 | 172 | 1 | | |
| Shiva Dance Dance Dance | 5 | 173 | 1 | • | |
| Om Namo Gurudev Namo | 5 | 174 | 1 | | |
| Jai Ganesh | 5 | 174 | 1 | | • |
| Twameva Maata | 5 | 187 | 1 | | |
| O God Beautiful | 5 | 189 | 1 | | |
| Om Shanti | 7 | 242 | 1 | | • |

| Buddhist | Ch | P | MF | D | CH |
|---|---|---|---|---|---|
| Om Tara Tu Tara | 4 | 139 | 1 | | |
| Kwan Zeon Bosai | 4 | 139 | 1 | | |
| Gate, Gate | 5 | 176 | 1 | | • |
| Om Mane Padme Hum | 5 | 176 | 1 | | • |
| Buddham, Saranam, Gaccami | 5 | 177 | 1 | | |
| Padma Sambava Mantra | 5 | 177 | 1 | | |
| May All Beings Be Well | 7 | 244 | 1 | | • |

| African | Ch | P | MF | D | CH |
|---|---|---|---|---|---|
| Ib Aché (eeb ashay) | 1 | 11 | 1 | | |
| We Come From de Water | 2 | 59 | 2 | | |
| Eewa Beleyo– Pygmy Elephant Song | 3 | 82 | 1 | | • |
| Ancient Mother | 4 | 117 | 1 | | |
| Man Gwa Nem | 4 | 126 | R | | |
| Yemaya Asesu | 4 | 141 | 1 | | |
| Thula Klezio (Nhliziyo) | 7 | 226 | 1 | • | • |
| Asite Dumayla | 7 | 231 | 1 | • | • |
| Bon Ca Va a de Kele | 7 | 232 | 1 | | |
| Freedom is Coming | 7 | 248 | 2 | | |
| Kwaheri | 7 | 262 | 1 | | |

| Other | Ch | P | MF | D | CH |
|---|---|---|---|---|---|
| Ungala We (Australian/Aboriginal) | 1 | 11 | 1 | • | • |
| Terre Rouge (French) | 2 | 29 | 1 | | • |
| Hotaru Koi (Japanese) | 2 | 39 | 1 | | |
| She Will Bring The Buds in Spring (Eng. Trad.) | 3 | 76 | 1 | | |
| Be Like A Bird (Eng. Trad.) | 3 | 86 | R | | |
| As the Swan Sings (Eng. Trad.) | 3 | 87 | R | | • |
| Ehara ( Maori) | 3 | 93 | 1 | | |
| Isla Mujeres (Spanish) | 4 | 115 | 1 | | |
| Ek Ong Kar (Sikh) | 5 | 175 | 1 | | |
| Ahura Mazda (Zoroastrian) | 5 | 186 | 1 | | |
| En Lak' Ech /A Lak'en (Mayan) | 5 | 190 | 1, CR | | |
| 'Tis a Gift to be Simple (Shaker) | 6 | 197 | 1 | | • |
| Love, Love, Love (Eng. Trad.) | 6 | 207 | R | | • |
| O Dear Friend (Eng. Trad.) | 6 | 208 | 1, C | | • |
| What Wondrous Love (Quaker) | 6 | 210 | 1 | | |
| If the People Lived Their Lives (Russian) | 7 | 238 | R | • | |
| Ele Ele Tau Mai (Hawaiian) | 7 | 246 | 1 | • | • |
| For Food and Joy (Greek) | 7 | 254 | R | | • |
| Let's Be Beginning(German) | 7 | 233 | R | | • |

# About the Author

    Kate Marks received her M.S.W. (Masters of Social Work) from the University of California at Berkeley in the mid–sixties where she began her exploration of different spiritual paths and became deeply involved in holistic health, feminism and the human potential movement. She has trained extensively in body-centered, expressive therapies, vibrational/ sound healing, polarity therapy, meditation, shamanism and ritual arts. She has travelled widely and studied with many teachers and native medicine people. She was initiated into Sufism by Pir Vilayat Inayat Khan in 1971.

    As a singer, drummer and ceremonial guide, she also leads sacred song, dance and ritual circles, facilitates women's empowerment groups and rites of passage. She has a private practice in Western Massachussets and gives workshops in the U.S. and Europe.

FOR INFORMATION AND WORKSHOPS CONTACT:

Full Circle Press
P.O Box 428
Amherst, MA 01004